Chambers
SCOTTISH
FOOD BOOK

Chambers
SCOTTISH
FOOD BOOK

with recipes by Jack Gillon
and text by Jenny Carter and Janet Rae

Acknowledgments

Scotland is rich in homegrown food, its fields, rivers and surrounding seas regularly yielding abundant harvests of meat and fish, grain, fruit and vegetables. An appreciation of this abundance is all the more enhanced by talking to the men and women who work in the food industry. Many of these people have contributed generously of their time to make this book possible and for this the authors are deeply grateful.

Thanks are also due to Mr John Leese of the British Farm Produce Council, to Mrs M. Bowman for permission to quote 'Root Crops' by her late husband, Derek Bowman, and researchers Patricia Kane, Jennifer McWilliam and Lucinda Gray. Additionally the authors would like to thank Thérèse Duriez for editing the manuscript, Bill Rae for correcting the proofs and Alastair Fyfe Holmes of Chambers for helping make the project a reality.

Finally, we are indebted to Macdonald Publishers, Edinburgh, for permission to reproduce the drawings by Alison Gow on pages 21, 24, 25, 29, 36, 37, 41, 55, 71, 72, 73, 74, 77, 92 and 104, and to Harriet Wylie for the drawings on pages 40, 42, 52, 53, 56, 57, 58, 76, 93, 102, 103, 112, 113, 120, 121, 122 and 123.

© Jack Gillon, Jenny Carter and Janet Rae 1989

Published by W & R Chambers Ltd Edinburgh, 1989

British Library Cataloguing in Publication Data

Chambers Scottish food book.
   1. Food: Scottish dishes.   **2. Food: Scottish dishes – Recipes**
   I. Gillon, Jack, *1949–*
   641.3'009411

ISBN 0 550 20001 0

Produced by Carter Rae Editorial Services
Design and layout by F.M. Artwork and Design
Typeset by Hewer Text Composition Services
Colour origination by Bordercolour, Brampton, Cumbria
Printed by The Eagle Press PLC

Contents

Introduction

Traditional Scottish cooking has been amply documented. All of the many authors who have been drawn to the subject have provided a fascinating and evocative view of the past. The recipes themselves constitute a sort of social, political and psychological history of our nation. Perhaps because of this, they are for the most part rather prosaic. There are no interesting or useful recipes for salmon, and precious few for beef, lamb or game, possibly indicating that those who could afford them preferred simple methods of cooking. The best of the traditional recipes are undoubtedly those which bear the hallmark of the Auld Alliance with France. Often the names of these dishes can be traced back to the French, but just as often a certain French influence, or an echo of a specific French recipe, can be found in dishes which we think of as being characteristically Scottish. Many French queens and their courtiers have left their mark on the kitchen.

No culinary tradition can exist in a fossilised state. French cooking is the undisputed leader precisely because it has always been amenable to change and development, from the introduction by Catherine de Medici of important Italian recipes to the recent *nouvelle cuisine* revolution. If we are to claim that there is a worthwhile Scottish cuisine we must find convincing and interesting things to do with our much vaunted natural produce, drawing on the many influences which have changed people's attitudes to food in recent times, and on what we have learned from the immigrant populations now living among us and sharing their traditions with us. Even so, we must acknowledge that a Scottish cuisine should be rooted in our climate and psyche. Scottish food, to be recognisable as such, should be straightforward and warming, simple perhaps, but conceived with the flair and passion which characterise the Scottish temperament.

The starting point must be the quality of the raw ingredients. Food shopping in Scotland was a dispiriting business until very recently, but now we have once again the opportunity to capitalise on all the fine things our land produces. Nothing in these pages is difficult to find in the cities, and most can now be found even in small towns. It is impossible to know to what extent these changes have been consumer driven, but there is no doubt that foreign travel, higher disposable incomes and a widespread sense of the health and pleasure to be obtained from good eating have combined to stimulate the markets to deliver the necessary materials for this burgeoning interest. The power of a crusading band of media 'foodies' has undoubtedly been another factor.

Those who produce the foods we want, and the authorities who govern their production, have not always responded to the wishes of the public and the food trade with enthusiasm or alacrity. While membership of the European Economic Community has been a major beneficial influence in breaking down barriers both fiscal and psychological, it has brought in its train a series of legislative actions which have forced change on our traditional methods of food production, and not always for the better.

In this book we have set out to describe and analyse this evolutionary process. For the first time since World War II, and perhaps longer, there is a vibrant interest in food throughout the land, and a food industry motivated to service this interest. Producers, cooks and eaters alike are aware not only of the good things of our heritage, but also of its deficiencies. However the gaps and weaknesses in our traditional cooking and eating patterns have arisen, at least we now know how to redress them. We are discovering that we had forgotten much – that herbs and garlic were common in years gone by, that fish and shellfish were once more widely consumed than meat, and so on.

Our memory has been jogged not only by bookish writers and foreign travel, but also by individuals who have been drawn to produce the sorts of foodstuffs which we think of as foreign, but which were once common here. Vegetables and herbs

Opposite: Growing courgettes at Ken Paterson's Simply Organic Farm.

(Della Matheson)

7

not so long ago considered exotic are being grown in our fertile alluvial soils, and by the best, small-scale methods. Hand-made cheeses are reappearing. Some are new, others like Humphrey Errington's Lanark Blue, revive a lost art. Both enrich our national culture as much as our palates.

It is doubtful whether a genuine national style of cooking is possible in this post-modern, post-nouvelle era. From a Scottish viewpoint the most significant shift in the very recent past has been into the post-*Taste of Scotland* age. Tourists and natives are too sophisticated nowadays to be fooled by a tartan-clad museum piece of a dish, badly executed and overpriced. Restaurateurs are cooking with more skill and imagination, and are assimilating the concepts and techniques of other cultures without losing the character and flavour of our natural produce. Freshness and simplicity are the hallmarks of good modern cooking. Perhaps directness is a better word than simplicity, for the end results can be complex and satisfying when the methods used are straightforward and easily mastered. It is notable that whereas in days gone by the home cook could never emulate the dishes served in restaurants because of problems of scale, the boot is now firmly on the other foot. The best restaurants now cook on a domestic scale, with many dishes being cooked individually and only assembled on receipt of an order. This is as it should be, and a major benefit is that the restaurant customer increasingly understands the dish before him or her, putting pressure on chefs and hoteliers to provide food in tune with the tastes and sensibilities of the people.

The home cook now has an unprecedented opportunity to explore and recreate the national larder. This book has been conceived as a guide to this voyage of exploration. The text traces the development of food production and eating patterns from centuries back up to the present day. Similarly the recipes are conceived as an overview of the methods which will lead to a modern style of cookery while allowing the qualities of our national produce to emerge. There are, of course, some splendid traditional recipes which must not be consigned to the scrap heap, but it is not the purpose of this book to catalogue them. I have included only those which remain modern in spirit, or which illustrate a particular point. This is most clearly seen in the chapter on baking, in which originality is more likely to consist in using the traditional methods and recipes in new ways than in genuine invention.

More often, however, I have used a traditional recipe as a point of departure. The modern versions are not necessarily better, but they are perhaps more in tune with our times, and of course it would be entirely in keeping with the spirit of these times if the recipes prove to be ephemeral. With practice, the methods I use and describe in this book become second nature. Somehow this style of cooking leads to inventiveness. It is based on respect for the appearance, texture and flavour of the best food that our plentiful land can provide.

Jack Gillon

Recipe Reference

First Courses

Main Courses

Vegetable Dishes

Desserts

Cakes, Breads and Bannocks

Pastry

Sweets and Preserves

Table of Equivalent Measures – English/American

An American measuring cup holds 240ml. (8 liquid ounces), an American half pint. Dry ingredients measured in cups will vary in weight according to the density of the ingredient. Some equivalent measures are given below:

450g. (1lb.) flour = 4 cups sifted flour
225g. (½lb.) sugar = 1 cup
225g. (½lb.) butter = 1 cup

1. Fish-The Perennial Favourite

'It's herring, boys! Herring! Herring!'

They forgot all about the ship; they forgot everything, except the herrings, the lithe silver fish, the swift flashing ones, hundreds and thousands of them, the silver darlings.[1]

In a land blessed with rich seas, lochs and streams, it is hardly surprising that fish has featured in Scotland's cuisine for centuries. 'In Argyllshire you have the Loch Fyne herring, fat, luscious and delicious, just out of the water, falling to pieces with its own richness – melting away like butter in your mouth. In Aberdeenshire you have the Finnan haddo' with a flavour all its own, vastly relishing – just salt enough to be piquant, without parching you with thirst. In Perthshire there's the Tay salmon, kippered, crisp and juicy – a very magnificent morsel . . .' writes F. Marian McNeill in her classic book *The Scots Kitchen*.[2] 'Indeed,' says McNeill, 'so plentiful was the fish [salmon] that it was despised by the upper classes, and farm hands used to stipulate that it should not be served to them more than so many times a week.'[3]

Fish was plentiful, cheap and nutritious, and 'apart from its nutritional value and tastiness, it was a common cure for sickness.'[4] The tradition of fishing goes back a long way in Scotland, a country with a massive coastline, fine sea-lochs and freshwater streams. The Vikings in the eighth century brought with them their experience of the sea, and the Scots took up fishing in a more organised way. A hundred years later fishermen from Fife had found the secret of curing fish in salt, panned from the sea, and the country gained a reputation for its fresh, smoked and pickled fish. By the fifteenth century bitter disputes about fishing rights had begun with the Dutch and the continuation of disputes to the present are an indication of the importance of fishing to the economy.

The Fisheries Board for Scotland was established in 1807 to inject economic life into fishing and establish a system of controls. All through the nineteenth century there was a high demand for Scots white herring, particularly from export markets. Herring went to the Baltic, to the West Indies (where planters bought the fish for their slaves) and to Ireland and England. Shellfish, too, were popular, and crabs, mussels, lobsters, scallops and oysters were in high demand.

The 1850s to 1880s were boom years – but in 1884 the 'silver darlings' failed the fishermen, and within two years shipwrights and coopers, as well as fishermen, had been forced out of business. And although the fish returned within a few years, fleets were reduced and demand never peaked in quite the same way again. The Depression which followed World War I hit fishermen particularly hard – there were few ships, no money for investment, markets changed. Now, in the late 1980s, demand for fish is again high, and world-wide; but deep sea fishing by British vessels is more or less at an end. Limited by the 200-mile (322-km.) territorial restriction, boats can no longer fish off Iceland and Greenland where cod is so plentiful. In addition, EEC legislation has affected Scottish fishing and until the revision in 1983 of the fishing agreement of 1964 (adopted before Britain's entry to the European Economic Community) overfishing was a major problem. Indeed, despite the new agreement, sonar equipment, trawl nets and purse seine-nets can work all too efficiently, particularly in the case of herring with their seasonal migration routes and well-documented diurnal habits. In 1977 the North Sea Herring Fishery had to be closed, and the following year a ban was imposed on the West Coast grounds. Although the market is open once more and herring are plentiful again, demand has shrunk and now a high percentage of sales goes to Eastern Europe.

Previous page: A fishing boat returns to Ullapool.
(Highlands and Islands Development Board)

Gutting the herring at Peterhead. Gutting was a skill which called for 'great speed and dexterity'.

(The Scottish Fisheries Museum Trust Ltd)

Over the last ten or fifteen years, the industry has seen major changes. A tightening up of controls throughout the EEC has meant the enforcement of high standards. Laws govern net mesh sizes and conditions of use, the definition of areas which can be fished, the minimum size of fish, crustaceans and molluscs, seasonal restrictions, hygiene regulations, and fish farming. Apart from the influence of EEC legislation and the imposition of quotas, there have been big advances in freezing technology. Fish caught at peak condition and properly frozen will maintain a high quality – better, in fact, than the so-called 'fresh' fish of the past. Other bodies – the Sea Fish Industry Authority and the Highlands and Islands Development Board – have done much by way of promotion. The SFIA's 'Sea Fish Quality Award' scheme was designed to give housewives a guide to quality. Fishmongers displaying the symbol are 'indicating that their premises, product and handling practices exceed the minimum standards laid down by law.' Guides for shoppers have been introduced, giving information about what to look for and generally promoting 'one of the purest and most nutritious foods we can eat.'

It all seems a long way from the picturesque old days when girls worked in teams – two gutters and one packer, supported by coopers. With great skill they slit the throat, removed the guts, then 'roosed' the fish (salted and turned them) before packing them for transportation. One man describing these girls in the 1930s spoke of their:

> . . . great speed and dexterity. With one movement of their sharp knives the herring was split and the guts shot into a bin. Another flick of the wrist sent the herring flying into one of the three troughs – first, second or third grade. A boy pivoted the bins towards the lorries waiting to take away the fish and the entrails. Scavenging gulls swooped down occasionally for leftovers. And the constancy and skill of the girls at work was almost mesmerising: it excited comment.[5]

The fishing fleet at Wick drying its sails. Herring fishing reached its peak in Scotland between 1850 and 1880.

(Wick Heritage Centre)

Unloading fish for sale at Lochinver.

(Highlands and Islands Development Board)

At the same harbour – Stronsay – the pier-head market had 25 offices, and they could get very busy. 'For two hours of a Tuesday morning there would be a line of baskets 40 yards [36.5m.] long with fishermen waiting for their turn of the auctioneer.'[6] The scene may have changed, but visit the auction shed at Mallaig or Lochinver – or any other fishing port – and the action is much the same.

Perhaps one of the biggest changes, apart from fishing boats with all the latest technology, has been in the range of fish and shellfish available in Scotland. Yet despite the wide choice, 'Seven out of ten fish purchases for home consumption are either cod, haddock or plaice, and the odds are that they will be fried in crumbs,' says Bob Kennedy, Scottish Marketing Director of the Sea Fish Industry Authority. Monkfish, mackerel, grey mullet, hake, halibut, turbot, brill and sole figure in many good fishmongers' windows, while shellfish include lobsters, prawns,

mussels, scallops and oysters (usually from fish farms). The biggest success story has been the acceptance of langoustine as a delicacy; until the 1960s scampi was regarded as a nuisance by British fishermen and thrown back.

Scottish fish has always been regarded as among the best in the world – cold water fish are regarded as having a better flavour and firmer flesh than fish from warmer seas. In the last five years expenditure on fish has risen considerably, and in Scotland consumption of fresh fish is high compared with the national average. 'This may be due to two factors,' says Bob Kennedy 'a historic reliance on fish, and the abundance of fresh fish in Scotland. One striking difference is the very heavy reliance in Scotland on haddock.' When haddock is scarce, Scottish consumption of fresh fish drops dramatically.

Changing legislation has meant changing fishing patterns, and now 40 per cent of fresh fish consumed in the United Kingdom is imported from Iceland, Norway and Denmark. A major new development has been the dramatic increase in the number of fish farms to compensate for the decrease in wild stock. The biggest port in Britain is now Peterhead, with Ullapool and Lerwick important in the herring industry (where tonnage is once again high, though prices remain low).

'Fresh herring will probably never quite regain its popularity,' comments Robert Thomson, Managing Director of Edinburgh fishmongers George Campbell and Sons. 'We do have some fresh trade in late spring and early autumn. Pickled herring and rollmops retain their popularity. Many kippers are now made using imported herring, although the Loch Fyne kipper is made with Clyde herring.'

A perennial favourite is salmon, either fresh or smoked, and the development of salmon farming in the last two or three years has been phenomenal. By early 1988 fish farms in Scotland numbered 400, with a total value approaching £100 million and actively doubling every year. Smolt (young river salmon) production trebled between 1986 and 1988,[7] while the same years saw salmon production more than double.[8] Most farmed fish are salmon and trout, with experiments in plaice, turbot and halibut. Intensive salt-water fish culture is used mainly for salmon, mostly in sheltered, tidal inshore sea-lochs off Western Scotland and the Northern and Western Isles. The salmon are raised in cages and fed on dry pelleted feeds. They are ready for market in 12 to 24 months. Freshwater fish culture is mainly used for rainbow-trout farming. The fish are raised in cages, in concrete 'raceways' or in lined tanks.

The Scottish Salmon Farmers Marketing Board was launched in February 1988 to manage the interests of the Scottish Salmon Growers' Association (SSGA) and the Shetland Salmon Farmers' Association (SSFA). Active promotions in Britain, France and the United States are planned to increase market penetration for Scottish salmon, emphasising its image of quality and health.

The massive increase in fish farms is not without its attendant problems, however. There has been much concern about the effect on the environment, largely from effluent from the farms. Problems of pollution in Norway's fiords have indicated that farmed fish demand a good flow of water, and that inland lochs such as Loch Fyne or Loch Awe may not be ideal. Money is therefore being invested in research and development projects to ensure that minimum damage is done to the environment and to examine ways of reducing furunculosis, a disease in salmon which loses the industry up to £10 million per year.

One of the greatest concerns in the

Fish farming, Loch Grimshader, Lewis.
(Highlands and Islands Development Board)

fishing industry remains poaching. Salmon are seriously endangered by illegal trapping through the use of dynamite and gill nets. These, used for coastal fishing, are spread over a large area – as much as two miles (three kilometres) – outside the legal nets. They are made of thin nylon monofilament which traps the fish painfully by the gills, and causes marking and bruising. Poachers trap any size of fish and thus do a great deal of damage to the breeding stock. Salmon poached from the River Forth alone are worth an estimated quarter of a million pounds a year, while the salmon catch from Scottish rivers as a whole has halved over the last twelve years.

Parallel to the enormous increase in demand for farmed salmon and trout has been a similar growth of interest in seafood.[9] Scotland's pure waters, particularly the West Highland lochs, are ideal for seafood production, and in fact most shellfish are indigenous to Scotland – lobster, King, Queen and Princess scallops, winkles, cockles, crawfish, squid, langoustine, brown crab, velvet crab, oysters and mussels. Much seafood is exported to the Continent and the US

Opposite top: Feeding the fish at a trout farm.
(Highlands and Islands Development Board)

Opposite bottom: Grading broodstock, Otter Ferry Salmon Farm, Argyll.
(Highlands and Islands Development Board)

Above: Filleting salmon prior to smoking, Achiltibuie.
(Summer Isles Foods)

Left: Spearing salmon, 1843. A print from W Scrope, 'Days and Nights of Salmon Fishing on the Tweed'.
(The Scottish Fisheries Museum Trust Ltd)

Opposite top: Prawn sorting, Mallaig.

(Highlands and Islands Development Board)

Opposite bottom: Crawfish – at one time thrown back, this seafood has become highly fashionable.

(Highlands and Islands Development Board)

Left: Shrimping in the Solway at the turn of the century.

(School of Scottish Studies)

Below: Hebridean oysters – a tasty morsel.

(Highlands and Islands Development Board)

either fresh or frozen, smoked or processed.

Top of the market are Loch Fyne oysters, renowned for their high quality and reliability. The King and Queen scallop are indigenous to Scotland; the Princess was developed at Ardtoe, and takes only one year to mature. When mature, they are about the size of a 50-pence piece and they have an attractive pink shell. 'Mussels are always popular,' says fishmonger Robert Thomson. 'They have a better shelf life if they are left in clumps, and they are very easy to cook and cheap.' A natural mussel bed produces spawn which settles on ropes laid by farmers. They are left to mature for about two years and are lighter and prettier than wild mussels. While some shellfish are being farmed successfully, others remain uneconomic. A 680g (1½lb.) lobster – right for the table – takes seven years to grow. Mature lobsters are 30 years old.

Modern methods of preserving fish – notably freezing – are highly effective. But they do not impart a new character to the flesh, as do the more traditional methods. F. Marian McNeill described some of these in her inimitable style:

They may be sun-dried or rizzared (Fr. *ressoré*), wind-dried, or rock-dried, or

Filleting salmon, Kinlochbervie, in preparation for smoking.
(Highlands and Islands Development Board)

is gutted, filleted and brined for twenty minutes or more in a mixture of rum, molasses and juniper. Brining times vary – trout, eel and herring may be brined for about an hour, salmon for four to six hours depending on their size. It is then cold smoked at 20°C for 4 to 5 hours, or hot smoked at 50°C for an hour and finished at 80°C for ¼ hour. At Achilti-buie we use oak chippings from the cooperage at Invergordon. The whisky-soaked wood gives a very distinctive taste.

'We use wild salmon when available. It has a slightly firmer flesh which tends to cut better. But the quality of farmed salmon is very high. Fresh smoked fish has a shelf life of approximately six days; if it's vacuum packed, it can keep for twenty days.

'We have noticed the old folk around here like to cook their smoked salmon rather than eat it cold. They tend to grill it with a knob of butter.'

Salmon has not yet become so common, however, that it is once again rejected as tedious.

1. Neil M. Gunn, *The Silver Darlings*, Faber and Faber Ltd, London, 1941.
2. F. Marian McNeill, *The Scots Kitchen*, Blackie and Son, London and Glasgow, 1929 (1961 edition), p. 73.
3. *Ibid.*, p. 20.
4. Catherine Lucy Czerkawska, *The Fisherfolk of Carrick*, Molendinar Press, 1975, p. 33.
5. William Gibson, *The Herring Fishing – Stronsay*, vol. 1, BPP, 1984, p. 31.
6. *Ibid.*, p. 29.
7. From seven million to 21.69 million (Scottish Salmon Information Service).
8. 10 300 tonnes to an estimated 25 000, with an average of 1000 tonnes of wild river salmon in addition per year.
9. The five years between 1981 and 1986 saw a doubling of value of the seafood industry from £23.8 million to £46 million.
10. F. Marian McNeill, *The Book of Breakfasts*, Reprographia, Edinburgh, 1975, p. 80.

they may be smoked over peat, seaweed or aromatic wood. The most famous is undoubtedly the Findon (pronounced and usually misspelt Finnan) haddie, which takes its name from a hamlet six miles south of Aberdeen and which is inimitable on any other coast . . . The Moray Firth smoked haddocks have a very delicious flavour. Both Findons and Moray Firths are 'speldered' or split, whilst the Arbroath smokies, another excellent variety, with a flavour all its own, are cured whole.[10]

One of the oldest methods of preserving fish – smoking – remains the most popular. At Summer Isles Foods in Achiltibuie, north of Ullapool, Keith Dunbar explained the process they use: 'The fish

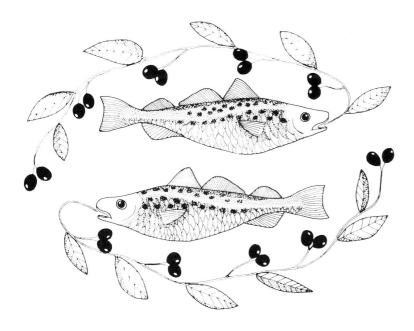

Halibut with Pepper Sauce

Halibut is a much misunderstood fish in Scotland, where there is a tendency to lump it with the proletariat of the seas, such as cod, haddock and the rest. It is, in fact, one of the great flat fish, on a par with turbot and Dover sole if it is dealt with kindly. For this recipe, and indeed for most others, flat steaks or escalopes cook better than the more usual transverse cuts across the bone. Try halibut, or turbot or brill, in the various salmon recipes described in this chapter.

Grind the peppercorns roughly, in whatever combination you prefer. Rub them into the fish steaks. Refrigerate the steaks while making the stock.

Make a stock with the fish bones and skin, carrot, onion, leek and fennel, the wine and an equal volume of water. Simmer for about 1 hour with some fennel, allowing the volume to reduce by half. Strain and reserve.

Sauté the steaks briefly in butter without browning. When barely cooked, remove from the pan and keep warm in foil parcels.

Deglaze the pan with armagnac or cognac, then add the juice of the lemon. Reduce to a golden essence.

Add the concentrated fish stock. Allow the sauce to amalgamate for a minute or two, then bring it back to simmering point. Off the heat, beat in chilled butter in small nuggets until the sauce is smooth and glistening.

Serve the steaks on a puddle of sauce. Plain, buttered new potatoes, fresh peas or asparagus are perfect companions.

For 6:

6 halibut steaks, each weighing about 100g. (¼lb)
black, white and Szechuan peppercorns
the fish trimmings
1 glass red wine
1 carrot
1 onion
1 leek
fresh fennel
50g. (2 oz.) butter
small glass cognac
1 lemon

Queen Scallops in a Light Vegetable Cream

Traditional Scottish fish soups tend to rely on a flour and butter roux for substance. This gives a hearty, rustic base, often accentuated by the choice of fish. Cullen Skink is the classic example, a good solid soup, sometimes thickened with mashed potato and flakes of smoked haddock. This concept can very easily be refined into a very delicate soup-cum-stew of virtually any fish. For extreme delicacy river fish (perch, trout, sea-trout) can be used, but scallops are unsurpassed for sweetness of flavour.

The first step is to make a good vegetable stock. Chop the vegetables and simmer in 900ml. (1½ pints) of water with the garlic, peppercorns and parsley, for no more than an hour.

Strain the stock into a clean pan. Add enough cream to give a good rich consistency, boiling down a little if necessary. Adjust the seasoning.

Add the scallops, coral included, with the butter, and simmer, stirring gently, for a few seconds only. Serve garnished with a few parsley or fennel leaves.

NOTE: If the queenies are very small, or if you are using fish cut into very thin strips, you can arrange them on the base of the soup plates in front of your guests. They will be perfectly cooked by the piping hot vegetable cream as soon as it is ladled over them. A sprinkling of saffron is visually attractive and quite delicious.

For 6 as a first course:

6–10 Queen scallops each person (or 2 large scallops)
2–3 carrots
2 sticks celery
1 medium onion
1 fennel bulb or 1 dozen fennel seeds
few slivers of garlic
few black peppercorns
good bunch of flat-leaf parsley
300ml. (½ pint) double cream
50g. (2 oz.) butter

Mussel and Onion Stew

This is an old Lothian favourite, for which the Doric Tavern in Edinburgh's Market Street has long been renowned. Nowadays the mussels almost invariably come from the West Coast. Any connection between the molluscs and the town of Musselburgh is a thing of the distant past – there are still plenty of mussels but because of the pollution in the Firth of Forth they cannot be used.

Scrub the mussels, removing the beard. Let them soak for several hours in 2 or 3 changes of cold water.

Put the mussels in a large saucepan with the wine. Bring to the boil and simmer, covered, until all of the mussels are open. This should only take a few minutes. Strain off the liquid and leave the mussels, still covered, in the pan.

In a saucepan make a flour and butter roux. Stir in the mussel liquid (being careful to leave the sand behind), making a smooth sauce. Add the milk gradually.

Chop the onion very fine and add it to the sauce. Simmer for 15 minutes. Adjust the seasoning if necessary.

Shell the mussels and add them to the sauce with the cream and chopped herbs. Heat through without boiling and serve immediately with plain, boiled rice and good bread.

For 6 as a main course:

1·5kg. (3lb.) mussels
1 large onion
50g. (2 oz.) butter
50g. (2 oz.) flour
600ml. (1 pint) milk
½ bottle dry white wine
300ml. (½ pint) double cream
parsley or chives
salt and pepper

Opposite: Halibut with Pepper Sauce.

(Victor Albrow)

23

Crab Soup (Partan Bree)

This is one of the best of our national dishes, sadly almost forgotten in home cooking. Partan is Gaelic for crab, and bree comes from the Gaelic *brigh* meaning juice. Crabs are now more easily available than they were just a few years ago, and present many possibilities apart from the standard 'dressed crab' – that is a wedge of lemon, a slice of tomato and some brown bread and butter. The traditional Partan Bree is equally simple, and this is perhaps its strength. It tastes of crab.

For 6:

1 large or 2 medium cooked crabs
100g. (4 oz.) pudding rice
600ml. (1 pint) milk
600ml. (1 pint) chicken stock
150ml. (¼ pint) cream
salt and pepper
anchovy essence or 2 anchovy fillets

Pick all the meat from the crabs and keep that from the claws separate.

Simmer the rice in the milk till soft. Pass it with the crab meat through a sieve.

Stir the mixture over a low heat till smooth, then gradually add the stock. Season with salt and white pepper. Add the anchovy essence to taste, or pound the anchovy fillets and mix in.

Bring the soup almost to simmering point, being careful not to let it boil. Just before serving add the meat from the claws and the cream.

Crab Soup–Modern Version

This is not necessarily better than traditional Partan Bree, but it is more interesting both in the cooking and in the eating. It is a variation on the French bisque – rich in texture and complex in flavour. Lobster or prawns can be treated in exactly the same way.

For 6:

1 large or 2 medium cooked crabs
1 stick celery or 1 leek
1 carrot
1 medium onion
225g. (½lb.) tomatoes
1 clove garlic
100g. (4 oz.) pudding rice
300ml. (½ pint) double cream (or mixture of double and single)
50g. (2 oz.) butter
1 15ml. spoon (1 tablespoon) whisky (or cognac or pastis)
2 15ml. spoons (2 tablespoons) fine herbs (fennel, or parsley, chives, tarragon or chervil in any combination)

Remove all the meat from the crabs, keeping the claw meat separate. Chop the shells and legs with a cleaver.

Chop the celery, carrot and onion roughly. Sweat these in butter without allowing them to colour. Add the crab shell, allowing it to be coated in butter.

Pour in the whisky and let it boil down a little.

Seed and chop the tomatoes, and add these with the rice and the garlic, finely chopped.

Top up with water, and simmer for 1 hour.

Remove any membranes from the coral, and add this with the soft, white meat to the soup.

Strain the soup through a sieve, pressing down well on the residue to extract flavour and as much purée as possible.

Return to the pan, add the cream and simmer until the consistency is smooth and fairly thick. Adjust the seasoning.

Just before serving, add the meat from the claws and the herbs, chopped very fine.

Little Pots of Sea-Trout in Jellied Cream

Potting in butter was a popular method of preserving trout, herring, shrimps and salmon. Here is a modern way of potting salmon, not to preserve it but to make an elegant first course. It is a derivative of the traditional Newhaven Cream, a forcemeat of smoked haddock or salmon with cream and eggs, traditionally served with a parsley sauce. The same method could be applied to smoked fish in a cream sauce – a solid Cullen Skink, in other words.

Put the fish bones in a pan with the vegetables, roughly chopped, add 600ml. (1 pint) water, season lightly and simmer for 1 hour, allowing the volume to reduce to almost 400ml. (2/3 pint). Strain the stock.

Fillet the salmon, leaving the skin attached. Bring the stock to the boil and plunge the two salmon fillets into it. Remove immediately from the heat and allow to cool gradually, then cool for an hour or so in a refrigerator, to see how much natural jelly is in the stock.

If the stock sets solid, rewarm gently, remove the salmon, skin it and break the flesh into large flakes.

Add double cream to the stock until it forms a rich, heavy sauce. Adjust the seasoning.

If the sauce sets in the refrigerator, add only about half of the gelatine dissolved in a little hot water. If it did not set, all of the gelatine may be required.

To test the consistency of the jelly, pour a little on to a saucer and chill for a few minutes, by which time it should be set. Add more gelatine if necessary, but do not overdo it – better that the finished dish be too soft than too rubbery.

When the sauce is almost cool, add the salmon, whole peppercorns and some chopped herbs and mix gently.

Oil the insides of individual ramekins and place a sprig of tarragon or fennel or a slice of peeled cucumber in the bottom of each. Fill each with the mixture and cool overnight.

Remove from the refrigerator an hour or so before serving. Warm the ramekins gently in hot water, and turn out on to individual plates. Serve with a salad of peeled, seeded tomatoes and blanched, diced cucumber, dressed with a lemon juice vinaigrette.

For 6 ramekins:

750g. (1 1/2lb.) sea-trout, on the bone (salmon is equally good)
fish bones (sole or turbot)
1 each of carrot, leek, onion and fennel bulb
150ml. (1/4 pint) of double cream
lemon rind
salt, black peppercorns
1 15ml. spoon (1 tablespoon) powdered gelatine
1 15ml. spoon (1 tablespoon) chopped herbs (parsley, tarragon, chervil or fennel)

Collops of Sea-Trout with Chanterelles

There is no word in English for chanterelles. These beautiful mushrooms grow in abundance in Scotland, among the moss, heather and blaeberries at the foot of beech trees. When I served this dish to some French friends I apologised for its seeming Frenchness, or lack of Scottishness. They were outraged. 'The fish is Scottish, the mushrooms are Scottish, the cook is Scottish and we are in Scotland.'

For 6:

1 sea-trout 1kg. (2 ½lb)
1 glass dry white wine
50g. (2 oz.) butter
450g. (1lb.) chanterelles (fresh or bottled)
2 shallots
300ml. (½ pint) of double cream
salt and pepper (white)
1 sprig fresh tarragon

To prepare the collops (escalopes):

Decapitate the fish and make a cut along the length of one side of the backbone. Prise flesh away from the bone, cutting cleanly through the transverse bones which stick out at the level of the lateral line. You will then have a 'side' of sea-trout.

Remove the transverse bones one by one with tweezers or thumbnail and knife.

To remove the skin: Place the fish skin side down. Separate skin and flesh at the tail and grasp the loose piece of skin, then run the knife confidently between skin and flesh, keeping the blade angled towards the skin. This must be done with a good knife on a flat surface.

Repeat the process on the other side. Divide each side into 3 equal portions.

To cook the collops:

Season the collops with salt and freshly ground white pepper. Place them in individual buttered foil parcels.

Sprinkle with dry white wine, add a few fresh tarragon leaves and a little extra butter to each parcel.

Seal the parcels tightly and bake in a hot oven (Gas 7, 425°F, 220°C) for 15 minutes.

To make the chanterelle sauce:

Trim the stems of the chanterelles. Wash briefly if necessary and dry thoroughly.

Fry them briskly in butter over a high heat. If they exude a large quantity of liquid, boil it down rapidly without stewing the mushrooms.

Add the shallots, finely chopped. Season carefully. Pour on enough cream to make a thick sauce.

To serve:

Unwrap the parcels, pouring any liquid into the sauce. Make a pool of sauce on each plate, and place the escalopes carefully in the centre, decorated with a few tarragon leaves. Fresh peas, or pea and spinach moulds, are the perfect accompaniment.

Opposite: Collops of Sea-Trout with Chanterelles.
(Victor Albrow)

26

Herring Roes in Puff Pastry with Mustard Sauce

Alan Davidson's *North Atlantic Seafood* is essential reading for anyone interested in cooking or eating fish. Most of the Scottish recipes he gives are for the 'offal' parts – heads, liver, roes, even swim-bladders. These were the fishermen's and the fishwives' for the taking, after the fish had been filleted and sun dried or salted for transport to the mainland. It follows that the majority of such recipes come from the islands, like the Crappit Heids (stuffed heads) from Shetland. The passing of most of these is not to be mourned, but soft herring roes are exquisitely delicate and sadly neglected. Look for them between April and June. If roes are not to be had, use herring fillets, cut into strips and treated in exactly the same way.

For 6 (as a first course):

450g. (1lb.) soft herring roes
2 15ml. spoons (2 tablespoons) prepared
 mustard
1 15ml. spoon (1 tablespoon) olive oil
freshly ground pepper
bunch fresh dill or fennel
450g (1lb.) home-made puff pastry (p. 102)

For the sauce:

300ml. (1/2 pint) home-made mayonnaise
2 15ml. spoons (2 tablespoons) single cream
1 15ml. spoon (1 tablespoon) lemon juice
1 15ml. spoon (1 tablespoon) prepared
 mustard
2 15ml. spoons (2 tablespoons) capers

Wash the roes briefly in cold water. Dry them in paper towels, and marinate in the olive oil, mustard, pepper and herbs for an hour or two.

Heat the oven to Gas 7, 425°F, 220°C.

Roll out the pastry. Cut it into 6 even shapes (squares or circles).

Put 1/6 of the roes on each shape, just off centre. Fold over and seal the edges tightly by indenting with the point of a knife. Make a small hole in the top of each.

Brush with beaten egg and bake on a greased tray for 20 minutes, by which time the pastry should be golden brown.

Mix the ingredients of the sauce, thinning with a little water if necessary. Serve with the hot pastries, garnished with the capers. Green salad provides a refreshing contrast.

Salmon Roasted in its Skin with Red Butter

The novelty in this dish lies not in the sauce, which is a reduced red wine stock enriched with butter, and is therefore similar to others described in these pages, but in the method of cooking the salmon. The crisp skin is the whole point. Many other sauces could be substituted, for example a hollandaise or herb butter.

For 6:

3 thick middle-cut salmon steaks
50g. (2 oz) butter
2 15ml. spoons (2 tablespoons) olive oil
1 onion
1 carrot
1 leek
fresh thyme
1/2 bottle red wine
salt, black pepper, lemon rind

Remove the flesh from each side of each steak, leaving the skin attached. Remove any small bones with tweezers. Coat the steaks with olive oil and black pepper, and refrigerate until needed.

Make a stock with the wine and vegetables, adding the thyme and lemon zest. Allow the volume to reduce by two-thirds. Strain, adjust the seasoning and reserve.

Fry the salmon steaks skin side down in a heavy frying pan which will transfer to the oven, until the skin is crisp. This will take only a few minutes.

Roast the salmon in a very hot oven (Gas 8, 450°F, 230°C) for 10 minutes only. They may rest in a warm place, covered, for 5–10 minutes.

Bring the sauce back to simmering point. Away from the heat, beat in cold butter until the sauce thickens and glistens. Serve on hot plates with new potatoes in parsley butter.

Collops of Salmon in a Green Vest

This dish looks more Irish than Scottish. Spinach, sorrel and cooked lettuce all combine particularly well with fish, and the method is equally applicable to firm white fish such as turbot or halibut.

Collops (from the French, escalopes) are flattish, thick slices cut from the fillet, with the skin removed (see p. 26 for method) but any shape will do as long as it is boneless and skinless and of a size suitable for a single serving. Quantities are unimportant – the volume of sauce can be adjusted with stock or cream as necessary.

Make a simple stock by simmering the skin and bones of the salmon with the wine, half of the leek and half of the onion, both roughly chopped, topped up with 300ml. (½ pint) water and seasoned, for 20 minutes. Strain and transfer to a clean saucepan.

Wash the outer leaves of the lettuce and an equal quantity of the largest spinach or sorrel leaves (about 4 leaves in total for each escalope). Soften them in the simmering stock. Drain and cool.

Season the escalopes with salt and freshly ground white pepper. Wrap each with a layer of sorrel or spinach, then a layer of overlapping lettuce leaves.

Chop the remaining onion and leek very fine. Soften them in butter in a heavy saucepan. Stir in the rest of the lettuce and spinach or sorrel, shredded. Add the stock and simmer over a low heat for 10 minutes, or until the vegetables are well cooked.

Blend the sauce, thinning with stock if necessary, and transfer it to a covered sauté pan big enough to take the salmon in a single layer (or two smaller pans).

Bring the sauce just to simmering point. Add the salmon parcels and cook covered for a few minutes, until the flesh is just resistant to the touch.

Place each escalope in the middle of a heated plate, with a knob of parsley butter on top.

Swirl the remaining butter into the sauce with a handful of chopped parsley (preferably flat-leafed), and pour some of the sauce around – not over – each escalope.

As always, the best accompaniment to salmon is buttered new potatoes, served separately.

For 6:

6 escalopes of salmon, each weighing about 100g. (¼lb.)
1 large lettuce (Cos or Webb, not Iceberg)
225g. (½lb.) spinach or a large bunch of sorrel
1 leek
1 small onion
50g. (2 oz.) butter
½ glass dry white wine
salt and white pepper

2. Game - No Longer Exclusive

See! from the brake the whirring pheasant springs,
And mounts exulting on triumphant wings:
Short is his joy . . .[1]

The richness of Scotland's native larder has long been a subject for comment. For a nation constantly drained by wars and poor in terms of hard cash, the lavishness of the table could often astonish visitors. Even the travelling folk, it seems, could produce a good game stew, though its origins might be suspect: 'It was, in fact, the savour of a goodly stew, composed of fowls, hares, partridges and moor-game, boiled in a large mess with potatoes, onions, and leeks, and from the size of the cauldron, appeared to be prepared for half a dozen people at least,' ran Scott's description of Meg Merrilies' cooking in

Guy Mannering. And if Meg's rich fare was undoubtedly poached, the princely hospitality shown by the Highland chiefs ('equalled only by their vanity,' commented Marian McNeill), certainly always included lavish displays of game from their lands.

Hunting on a grand scale was once a way of life:

And in the Highlands today [one can] hear the great tales of olden times: when the proud, high-antlered harts were the quarry of kings; when King James V, with twelve thousand men, killed eighteen score harts in Teviotdale and thirty score in Athole, along with roe and roebuck, wolf and fox and wildcat; when two thousand Athole men, gathering the deer in Mar and Badenoch, Athole and Murray, could

Opposite: A good grouse bag on the 'Glorious Twelfth' of August is still one of the highlights of the sporting year.
(Glyn Satterley)

Below: Deer farming on Jura. Farmed venison is of a consistently high quality.
(Highlands and Islands Development Board)

31

The annual shooting season was the highlight of the year and brought many wealthy Englishmen north to the Highlands.

(Highland Folk Museum)

drive a herd, numbering a beast for every man of them, to delight the eye of Mary Queen of Scots.[2]

Hunting has always been the sport of kings – or at least the very wealthy. In that respect, little has changed, and a day's shoot on a good estate can set you back many thousands of pounds. Stalking as a sport has only been practised for about two hundred years, and started after the deforestation of Scotland at the end of the eighteenth century.[3] It was, by some accounts, Cluny Macpherson, chief of the Clan Macpherson, who in 1745 was the first to stalk a deer on the Highland hillsides. Before that, culling was done at the *tainchell* at which many thousands of men and dogs took part, and concealed marksmen took a heavy toll of the deer.[4] Killing stags and hinds in a selective way during the open season remains the best way to keep the deer population healthy and under control, and strict laws now govern the sport. In the Highlands and Islands of Scotland alone the red deer population numbers about 180000, and an annual cull of some 30000 head is required.

While shooting and stalking remain the preserve of the wealthy, venison is nevertheless beginning to become a less expensive item for the average dinner-table thanks to the growth of deer farming. In 1974 the Rowett Research Institute in Aberdeen published *Farming the Red Deer*, which attracted wide publicity and led to the establishment of many deer farms in New Zealand and in Germany – but surprisingly few in Scotland. Nichola Fletcher has farmed deer at Reediehill, Auchtermuchty – Britain's first deer farm – since 1973. 'Farming deer is not really a revolutionary concept,' she said. 'From the middle ages deer were raised in parks, fish in fishponds and pigeons in dovecotes. They were all a ready supply of fresh meat in times when preserving carcases was extremely difficult. Deer were fed hay, apples or chestnuts. One account tells of a deer calf at Falkland Palace being hand reared on cows' milk.'

She is quick to extol the virtues of the meat. 'Venison is the least fatty and healthiest meat available,' she said, 'and if it is hung properly the meat is absolutely excellent. Venison is becoming very popular, but there are still only a few hundred tonnes being produced every year. There is no point in exporting venison as the home market consumes all that is produced. There is a little being imported from New Zealand.'

Venison from Reediehill is always from animals under three years old and, 'although it is expensive, it is consistently tender and succulent.' The deer are shot humanely at close quarters while grazing, not subjected to the indignities of an abattoir. Because the deer are kept in controlled conditions, farmed venison is consistent in quality while wild venison may come from old deer and be tough and stringy. 'Many of the fallacies about the necessity of long hanging and rich sauces stem,' says Nichola Fletcher, 'from Victorian times. The most prestigious heads were from old animals which, of course, needed long hanging and lengthy marinating in wines and spices to help to tenderise the meat.'

A high proportion of venison, both farmed and wild, goes straight to game butchers for retail. George Campbell and Sons in Edinburgh's Stafford Street sells 136–182 kilogrammes (300–400lb.) a week. But their trade in feathered game is perhaps even higher, and reflects the breadth of wildfowl available in Scotland: grouse, partridge (local and French), pheasant, woodcock, snipe, mallard and teal, wigeon and pintail.

'Most of the pheasants we sell are reared,' explained Robert Thomson, Managing Director. 'A good pheasant shoot with twelve guns out all day would provide about five hundred birds. We could take all of them. Most of our birds come from estates around Edinburgh.'

Campbells have a factory at Granton, Edinburgh, where they dress their game. Plucking and dressing are all done by hand, and the birds are sorted into categories, young and old. 'Plucking by hand you have to know which way the feathers go. If you don't, you tear the skin. By machine, you just have to adjust the position of each bird and it does the plucking for you. We always hang our

birds and try not to sell them until the week after they are shot because the meat is really quite tough. The fuss about the 12 August is really quite a nonsense – birds should not be shot and eaten on the same day. It takes a very clever person to cook grouse on the day that it was shot.' Most of the chefs in Edinburgh's hotels and restaurants now keep game off the menu until a week after the season starts. 'The gamekeeper comes in useful – he can tell you the age of a bird. Young birds can be roasted, but if you try to roast an old bird, it could come out like a cannonball. Old birds should be casseroled.'

'Game shooting is one of the most important attractions Scotland has to offer,' says James Farquhar, Factor to the Earl of Mansfield at Scone Palace, whose Logiealmond Estate runs to about 12 100

Wildfowling on Westray with snap net, cubbie and rope.
(School of Scottish Studies)

hectares (30000 acres), of which 3844 are on heather hill. Red grouse are not found anywhere else in the world, and form an important export. Game shooting and rearing is an incredibly involved subject. Pheasant can be reared, and here several thousand six- or seven-week-old pheasants are put into relief pens in the woods and are then looked after by the gamekeepers. They are fed on a mixture of feed, similar to poultry feed, starting with a very high protein type of meal which is pelleted. After a few weeks, most people would then introduce wheat and possibly maize; as the birds grow in size, so the amount of hard grain increases in relation to the pellets, until the birds are thirteen weeks or so when they are beginning to feed themselves and are able to fly and wander away from the relief pen. The gamekeeper's job then becomes considerably more difficult. He wants to keep them under control in the wood close to where the shooting takes place. He will try various different ways of protecting them from the elements and from foxes, and will feed them once or twice a day. He will also train them to come back to the pen when he whistles.

'Shooting is governed by statute. Pheasants are shot between 1 October and the end of January. Not many people shoot pheasants in October – they usually wait until November because wild pheasant will not rear their young up to an age where the young pheasant is capable of flying a suitable distance over a line of shooters. You cannot just go out and shoot a pheasant every day of the week because they will get frightened and disappear. Most people leave a gap of ten days to a fortnight between shoots.

'Grouse are totally different. They are entirely wild and no-one has managed to rear them successfully on the open hill. The whole business of shooting on a grouse moor is totally different too. Their shooting season is between the "Glorious Twelfth" of August and 10 December. Grouse are encouraged in their natural habitat, which is heather, by the management of an extensive area of hill ground to create an atmosphere where as many pairs

of grouse as possible can live in harmony and rear their young. The more peace and quiet they get from man, beast and bird, the better.

'At Logiealmond, there is a population of blue hare (hill hare) which is much smaller than the brown hare. They turn white in the winter, and we shoot them a lot in February and March.'

Rabbits, like pigeons, may be shot at any time of the year, because they are classed as vermin. Farmers often invite shoots on to their land to rid them of rabbit when young crops are growing. Lord Home writes, 'When cartridges were cheap, and the rabbit population so plentiful as almost to represent a plague, ferreting or driving the rabbits across narrow woodland rides was the best possible training for handling a gun.' His keepers at Douglas would trap thirty thousand couple a year, as well as culling the mountain hares:

> On a February day when the hares have turned white the cavalry charge up the hill is a spectacular sight, but shooting them is a duty rather than a pleasure. There is only one way to shoot the brown hare with any enjoyment, and that is to drive the ploughs and the grasses on a cold and frosty February day. Then they really go mad and gallop flat out, and the shooting is quick and clean.[5]

While in the Lowlands rabbits constituted a pest, one writer discussing life in a Highland glen noted:

> The rabbit, unknown north of the Tay until the nineteenth century, was something of a novelty when it was first introduced . . . It was some time before their nuisance value was really appreciated. The rabbit explosion had quite a serious effect on hill farming. It meant not only a loss of precious pasture but the ground was fouled as well, and farmers discovered that sheep would not graze where rabbit infestation was high.[6]

Pigeons, which have found favour in recent years as a delicacy for the table,

were introduced to Scotland as a source of meat when the overwintering of cattle was impossible. Before the introduction of the turnip in the eighteenth century (see chapter 3), cattle were habitually slaughtered. Pigeons or 'doos' (doves) were reared in 'doocots', and yielded a ready supply of fresh, tasty meat. The legacy of the habit may be seen around the country in the many elegant and pictures-que dovecotes to be found, often in the grounds of castles and country mansions.

Game farming has changed the exclu-sive nature of supply, and now there are many good game butchers who sell every-thing from venison to small game birds.

Perhaps this very traditional feature of high quality Scottish hospitality will now begin to recover a widespread popularity.

Returning home, north west Sutherland.

(Glyn Satterley)

1. Pope, from 'Windsor-Forest'.
2. David Stephen, *Highland Animals*, Inverness, 1974, p. 8.
3. G. Kenneth Whitehead, *Deer Stalking in Scotland*, Percival Marshall and Co., London, 1964, p. 1.
4. *Ibid.*, p. 1.
5. Lord Home, *Border Reflections*, Collins, London, 1979, p. 88.
6. Pat Thomson, *Take One Glen – recipes from glen kitchens*, Montrose, 1973, p. 24.

Roast Pigeon with Port and Tarragon

Pigeon is the most undervalued of game. When cooked rare it is surprisingly tender, with a rich, meaty flavour. They are so cheap that it is justifiable to use only the breasts. The carcases will make a fine stock, ideal for a dish of braised venison or beef.

For 6:

6 plump wood pigeons
50–100g. (2–4 oz.) butter
1 glass port
small bunch fresh tarragon
salt, coarsely ground black pepper
wine vinegar or juice of a lemon

Trim and singe the pigeons. Smear the skin over the breasts with soft butter and sprinkle very liberally with coarsely ground black pepper.

Put a small knob of butter, a sprig of tarragon and a sprinkling of salt inside each bird.

Roast in a hot oven (Gas 7, 425°F, 220°C), breast uppermost, for 15 minutes.

Pour a little port into the cavity of each bird. Return to the oven, reduce the heat to the minimum setting, and leave the door ajar. Allow the birds to rest for 5–10 minutes at the most.

Remove the birds, pour all of the liquid from each back into the roasting pan. Add a little vinegar or lemon juice and boil vigorously. Finish the sauce by beating in small parcels of butter until the sauce is glistening and homogeneous.

Carve the breasts, slice neatly and serve coated with the sauce.

Roast Grouse with Blaeberries

Grouse is best cooked in exactly the same way as the roast pigeon with port and tarragon (above), except that the legs should be served, the tarragon omitted (thyme may be substituted) and a handful of blaeberries per bird added to the pan for the 5-minute rest period prior to carving. Finish the sauce by swirling in the butter off the heat, or alternatively thicken it with a little cornflour or arrowroot dissolved in port. Serve with a sweet purée of Jerusalem artichokes or peas with spinach.

Roast Wild Duck with Glazed Turnips

The larger game birds pose a particular challenge to the cook. The legs are best when well done, while the breast meat must be served rare. The following method is equally applicable to pheasant and wild goose. The legs, cooked separately, may be served with the breast meat, but are probably best reserved for a different, more rustic meal.

Remove the breasts from the duck *on the bone* by cutting along the ribcage with kitchen scissors and cutting through the wing joint so that the wing remains attached to the breast section.

Detach the legs and save them for another recipe, or grill them slowly if they are to be used. Chop up the carcase and giblets, and brown in a heavy saucepan in the oil or duck fat. Add the vegetables, roughly chopped. When they have taken colour pour in the vinegar and boil it down to almost nothing. Top up with water (about 600ml. or 1 pint), and simmer for an hour or two, aiming for a final volume of about 200ml. (⅓ pint). Strain and reserve.

Peel the turnips and cut into 5cm. (2-inch) wedges or ovals. Fry gently in a heavy pan in butter until they begin to brown, then pour in half of the Madeira. Raise the heat and allow to caramelise slightly.

Off the heat put the duck breasts in the same pan, over the turnips, skin uppermost. Brush with butter and season copiously with black pepper.

Roast the duck breasts in a hot oven (Gas 7, 425°F, 220°C,) for 20–25 minutes depending on size.

Remove the ducks and keep them warm. Pour off any excess fat, then add the rest of the Madeira. Next add the stock, bring to the boil, add the cream and simmer to thicken while you carve the ducks.

Carve each duck breast whole from the bone, then slice lengthwise into slivers. The meat should be pink and moist.

Arrange the meat in fan shapes on heated plates, garnished with the turnips and sauce. A potato gratin is a good accompaniment.

For 6:

2 or 3 wild duck, depending on size
450g. (1lb.) turnips (yellow or white)
25g. (1 oz.) butter
1 15ml. spoon (1 tablespoon) oil or 25g.
* (1 oz.) duck fat*
½ glass Madeira or port
150ml. (¼ pint) double cream
sprig of thyme
salt and black pepper

For the stock:

1 carrot
1 onion
1 leek or stick of celery
3 or 4 whole garlic cloves
1 15ml. spoon (1 tablespoon) wine vinegar

Pheasant Braised with Curly Kale in Walnut Oil

Pot-roasting is one of the simplest ways of keeping pheasant moist and succulent. Compare this recipe with the pot-roast of chicken with wild mushrooms (p. 58).

Loosen the skins of the pheasants and insert chopped parsley between skin and flesh. Season inside and out with salt and freshly ground black pepper.

Brown the pheasants evenly in walnut oil over a moderate heat (avoid overheating the oil, as this will spoil its flavour).

Put a clove of garlic inside each pheasant. Place them breast down in a deep, oven-proof casserole.

Wash the kale and dry it thoroughly (e.g., in a saladier). Turn it in walnut oil in the same pan, with the onion, finely sliced. Season, and arrange the kale around and over the pheasants.

Pour 1 cup of water into the base of the casserole without wetting the kale. Braise in a moderate oven (Gas 4, 350°F, 180°C) for 1–1½ hours, until the pheasant is quite tender.

Carve the pheasants and arrange on a platter, surrounded by the kale. Finish the sauce with cream and pour over. Decorate with parsley.

For 6:

2 pheasants
450g. (1lb.) curly kale (spring greens or Savoy cabbage can be substituted)
1 large onion
walnut oil
salt and pepper
2 cloves garlic
fresh parsley
75g. (3 oz.) double cream

Pheasant Breasts with Cèpes

Any game bird will do, and other wild mushrooms can be substituted, but a young pheasant with cèpes is the best that late autumn can offer.

Remove the breast sections from the pheasants on the bone. Reserve the legs for another recipe, leaving the rest of the carcase for the stock.

Fry the carcases in butter until brown. Add the vegetables, chopped roughly, and turn in the butter. Pour in the wine, add the garlic, dried cèpes, a few peppercorns and some parsley, and simmer for 1½–2 hours, topping up with a little water if necessary. Strain and reserve.

Slice the cèpes into thick slices. Fry them in butter with a little finely chopped onion or shallot until just browning and free of excess liquid. Season the cèpes and put them in the bottom of the roasting pan.

Force some butter and chopped parsley under the skin of the pheasant breasts. Brush the outside of the skin with butter, and season heavily with black pepper.

Put the pheasant breasts over the cèpes, skin uppermost, and roast in a hot oven (Gas 7, 425°F, 220°C) for 20 minutes.

Meanwhile deglaze the pan in which the cèpes were fried with the Madeira, allowing it to caramelise slightly. Pour in the stock and simmer while the pheasant is roasting until the final volume is reached. Thicken lightly with cornflour and stir in a little butter to enrich the sauce.

Carve the pheasant breasts and arrange on individual plates with the sauce. Sprinkle the cèpes with chopped parsley and place them in the sauce. Serve with individual potato gratins.

For 6:

2 pheasants
450g. (1lb.) cèpes (fresh or bottled)
2 carrots
1 stick celery
1 onion stuck with a clove
few cloves garlic
2 glasses wine
50g. (2 oz.) butter
25g. (1 oz.) dried cèpes
small glass Madeira (Malmsey or Bual)
salt, pepper, parsley, cornflour

Opposite: Pheasant Breasts with Cèpes.

(Victor Albrow)

Rabbit with Prunes in Red Wine

Rabbit is barely mentioned in traditional Scottish cookery books. The only recipe given by F. Marian McNeill is for curried rabbit of all things. Properly cooked, a rabbit can be a great pleasure to eat. Braised or stewed, wild rabbit develops a very distinctive flavour which takes me back to boyhood and the days before myxomatosis, when rabbit was part of our everyday fare. Now they are plentiful again, and still very cheap.

As with hare, it is worth cooking the saddle separately. Try cooking the legs and shoulders according to the following recipe, cooking the saddles as in the hare recipe on p. 41, with shortened cooking times (it needs only a minute or two to fry in butter), adding a little mustard at the last minute. Serve the two versions with their respective sauces on one plate – it gives a fascinating contrast, and is as fine as anything you could wish.

For 6:

2 young rabbits
½ bottle red wine
1 large carrot
1 large onion
100g. (¼lb.) mushrooms
2 cloves garlic
50g. (2 oz.) butter
450g. (1lb.) large prunes
bay leaf, fresh thyme or oregano
salt, pepper, cornflour

Joint the rabbit and marinate the pieces overnight in the wine with the vegetables, roughly chopped, and the herbs.

Soak the prunes separately in a little of the wine.

Dry the pieces of rabbit, and brown them gently in butter in a heavy casserole.

Add the mushrooms, chopped, and brown them adding more butter if necessary.

Pour in the marinade, with the vegetables. Season and simmer for 1½ hours, or until the rabbit legs are just tender.

Remove the pieces of rabbit. Strain the sauce, and return it to the pan. Add the prunes, with the rabbit, and simmer for another 20–30 minutes.

Taste the sauce. If it is thin or sharp, add bramble jelly until the flavour is correct. Thicken with cornflour, and stir in the rest of the butter for enrichment.

Serve with boiled potatoes in chive butter.

Saddle of Hare with Beetroot and Chives

Fillet of hare, the meat from the saddle, is one of the finest delicacies. It is vandalism to stew it for hours with the legs and shoulders, so freeze these for less elegant occasions and use the fillets when fresh. Even when the hare is well hung the fillet will have a subtle and delicate flavour, provided it is cooked lightly. Nowadays you can often buy the saddle on its own, even in the large supermarkets.

In this recipe the saddle is cooked simply in a cream sauce. The freshly cooked, hot beetroot provides contrast in colour, texture and flavour.

Trim any membranes from the hare. Marinate in a little olive oil, lemon juice and coarsely ground black pepper for a few hours.

Prepare the mushrooms. If using dried cèpes, these must be soaked in a little water for at least 30 minutes.

Brown the hare saddles lightly in a little butter, over a moderate heat. Remove and keep warm.

Raise the heat and fry the mushrooms in the same pan, in a little extra butter. If using dried mushrooms, wring them dry first, reserving the fluid for the sauce.

Pour in the Madeira, still over a high heat, and when it has almost evaporated add the mushroom liquid or a little water (or game stock, if you have it).

Add the cream, and simmer until it is slightly thicker than single cream. Adjust the seasoning.

Wrap the fillets in individual foil parcels, adding a little sauce to each. Seal as hermetically as possible. Bake in a moderate oven (Gas 4, 350°F, 180°C) for 15 minutes at the most.

Meanwhile peel the beetroot and chop into 1·5cm (½-inch) thick cubes. Stew gently in a little olive oil until heated through. Add a splash of good wine vinegar and plenty of chopped chives, and season.

Remove the hare saddles and pour the sauce back into the pan. Take each fillet from the bone, carve it into 4 or 5 slices, and arrange these on the plate in a fan shape. Pour the reheated sauce around and place the beetroot so that it lies partly in the pool of sauce.

For 6:

3 hare saddles
100g. (¼lb.) fresh wild mushrooms, or 50g.
   (2 oz.) dried cèpes
25g. (1 oz.) butter
150ml. (¼ pint) cream
½ glass Madeira (Malmsey or Bual)
25g. (1 oz.) butter
450g. (1lb.) freshly boiled beetroot
olive oil, wine vinegar, lemon juice
1 bunch chives
salt, black pepper

41

Fillet of Venison Poached in a Madeira Sauce

Saddle of venison is fairly easily available, thanks to the success of deer farms. It is easier to cook than haunch, either roast on the bone (treat it like the fillet of beef (p. 54), or as fillets. These are slimmer than beef fillet, and require careful cooking. The results make it worthwhile. The sauce in this recipe can be made even more rich and complex by infusing blaeberries or brambles before poaching the fillets, or by adding wild mushrooms (fried in butter) just before serving.

For 6:

2kg. (4lb.) saddle of venison (on the bone)
600ml. (1 pint) good beef stock
1 glass Madeira (Malmsey or Bual)
25g. (1 oz.) butter
bouquet garni, bay leaf
salt, black pepper, cornflour

Remove the fillets from the bone. Marinate them in a little Madeira and black pepper.

Chop up the bones and brown them in butter in a deep casserole. Pour in the rest of the Madeira, then the stock, and simmer with the herbs for 1 hour. Strain the stock, and return it to the pan. Keep it at simmering point.

Brown the fillets, divided into several lengths if necessary, in butter over a high flame. Immediately poach them in the simmering stock for 10 minutes.

Drain the fillets, slice them on the bias and serve with the sauce thickened with cornflour and enriched with a little butter.

3. Meat - A Name for Quality

Some ha'e meat and canna eat
Some wad eat that want it;
But we ha'e meat and we can eat,
And sae let the Lord be thanket.[1]

The meat produced in the late eighteenth century, when Burns penned this grace, had none of the quality obtained from today's animals. In fact very little meat was eaten in the winter except the portion the farmer had salted. In the early 1700s, winter feed was so poor (often just straw and mashed whins – gorse) that it was the custom to slaughter most of the herd at Martinmas in early November when the grass had stopped growing. By spring the few animals that were able to survive the winter were often so weak they could barely walk to pasture. The practice in certain parts of the country of bleeding the cows, sometimes twice a year, only weakened them further. The blood, boiled and thickened with oatmeal, and then eaten with milk, added variety to the crofters' meagre diet, but the blood letting was hardly good husbandry.

The general improvement of agricultural land during the eighteenth century improved the quality of livestock. The introduction of the turnip revolutionised the keeping of cattle and sheep. At first the turnip was treated as a dessert and served with apples and oranges. Soon its value was realised – it grew late in the year and could be stored without rotting so it could be fed to cattle in the winter months. In addition the turnip cleansed the ground, replacing chemicals removed by grain crops. However as late as 1800 in Ayrshire, more than one-third of the cows and horses were still being killed off for want of winter fodder. Feedstuffs by this time also included rye grass and clover, and the weight and quality of both cattle and sheep benefited. The *Statistical Account* for the period, in recording Kinneff parish in Aberdeenshire, commented:

The parish rears a considerable number of black cattle; many more now than formerly. The great advance of price induces the farmer to rear four times the number of cattle which he raised 15 or 20 years ago; and his improved land enables him to feed

Previous page: Scots mutton pies – a traditional favourite.
(Scottish Tourist Board)

Right: An Arbroath butcher's shop in 1915.
(Dr Bruce Walker)

them on sown grass and turnips, until they are from two to three years old. He then finds a ready market and good prices, from his southern neighbours.[2]

All the farmers raise turnips for their cows and young cattle; and they in general are of opinion, that this is a more profitable way of using turnips than to feed cattle for the butcher. Cabbages in the field have been tried, but cattle always prefer turnips when they can get them.[3]

Though the quality of the animals improved only gradually, the Scots had a big trade in cattle and sheep with England. Many Highlanders would have been too poor to eat beef themselves: instead they sold their cows. Cattle 'trysts' (sales) were held regularly – one of the main centres was Falkirk – and drovers and their dogs moved cattle, in their tens of thousands, along the drove-roads southwards. The journeys were slow, and thieving commonplace. The beasts themselves needed shoeing – one smith along the way is said to have shod 30 000 head in one season. Nevertheless, the prices for the times were considered good: 20 000 head of cattle worth £130 000 were driven to England in 1794 from Dumfries, Wigtown and Kirkcudbright, the best bullocks (weighing 222·5kg., 35 stones) being sold for £8 each.[4]

Initially Scottish cattle were a mixed breed, though certain strains began to develop in different parts of the country. Highland cattle, perhaps the oldest of any breed in Britain, were particularly suited to the poor pasture and hills of the West Highlands. Descendants of these distinctive animals, with their curved horns and rust-coloured shaggy coat, are kept today solely for sentiment and as a tourist attraction.

The advent of the Highland and Agricultural Society in the 1800s placed new emphasis on breeding. The first Aberdeen Angus bulls and cows, the breed perhaps most identified with Scotland, were shown at Perth in 1829 by Hugh Watson of Keillor, near Coupar Angus:

Aberdeen Angus in the show ring at the Royal Highland Show.

(Carter Rae)

Mr Watson exhibited, and was awarded an extra premium for a lot of 10 Angus cows and heifers, bred by himself. One of the lot, a heifer afterwards exhibited at Smithfields, obtained there the medal in the class of extra stock. Her weight was estimated to be 130 or 140 stones [825 or 890kg.]. The bone of her foreleg was not thicker than that of the red deer, and her inside fat was equal to a quarter of her whole weight of beef.[5]

The Aberdeen Angus was not the only breed then being developed. Other farmers at this time were also working on strains such as the Scotch Shorthorn, Galloway, and Ayrshire. The Society also encouraged certain breeds of sheep: the Leicester, Cheviot and Blackface were those deemed most suitable for the demanding Scottish terrain.

In the early days, beef and mutton were usually salted and dried, the entrails being used for sausages stuffed with meal and suet. In the islands, crofters would band together to buy a cow or ox, to be butchered and salted for winter use. Meat was boiled with potatoes and turnips and kale; the poorer households considered roasting to be wasteful. The royal house-

*Most Scottish-produced lamb
goes South or overseas.*
(Della Matheson)

holds presented a stark contrast: the huge fireplace spits in Linlithgow Palace and Stirling Castle, could accommodate a whole side of an ox, while smaller spits were used to roast poultry and small special delicacies like quail, larks and finches.

In the Scottish diet pork has never figured as prominently as beef and mutton, and production has fallen in recent years. Twenty years ago, there were about 80 000 breeding sows in Scotland; that number has now been halved. Traditionally, fresh pork was not popular but people living in Edinburgh's Royal Mile sometimes kept a pig at the entrance to their tenements. In mid-nineteenth-century Shetland, pigs were often tethered by one leg in the kitchen. Small, hairy and brown, the Shetland pigs were turned out to root in the fields after the harvest, to fatten them for slaughter at Hallowmas, the feast of All Hallows or All Saints on 1 November. The pork that was

produced was initially salted or pickled. Later, when pig raising flourished further in regions like Ayrshire and Galloway, it was cured meat that became popular: although the pork pie is still considered very much an 'English dish', Ayrshire bacon occupies pride of place in many a Scottish breakfast and high tea.

The Scottish housewife has held to her preference for beef through the centuries, even if nowadays it tends to be more expensive than pork. The Scots consume 9kg. (20·4lb.) of beef per person each year, compared to the British average of 8kg. (17·6lb.). Despite the fact that so many sheep are grazed on Scottish hills, the Scots account for only 1·8kg. (3·9lb.) of lamb per head per year against the national average of 4kg. (8·7lb.). Pork consumption in Scotland stands at 2·5kg (5·7lb.) yearly compared to the national average of 4·5kg. (10lb.). (These figures are for household purchases only and do not take into account meat eaten outside the home – a growth area.)

'Scotland has built a reputation for quality beef,' says Alistair Donaldson, Chief Officer of the Meat and Livestock Commission (MLC), an organisation partly funded by statutory levies paid by farmers and slaughter houses. (The Commission's Scottish office is in Perth.) This is due to the fact that the production of beef in Scotland is based on the suckler herd, in contrast to the rest of Great Britain where beef is a by-product of the dairy herd. Good stockmanship and good grazing land also play an important part.

Although quality beef is readily available in Scotland, it is the cheaper cuts of meat that the Scottish housewife prefers. 'Fifty-five per cent of the beef bought in Scotland is used either in mince or stews,' says Mr Donaldson. 'The finer cuts – steaks and roasts – find ready outlets in the catering sector especially in London and the south-east.' Steak remains the most popular dish when eating out.

Scotland has traditionally exported 70 to 80 per cent of its lamb to the south and overseas: because of EEC price support levels, lamb production has actually increased and there is now in excess of four million breeding ewes in Scotland. In recent years, the production level of beef has slightly fallen. EEC quotas on dairy herds, and increased export of calves to the Continent, are partly responsible. Grazing, which was affected in 1985 due to poor weather, had improved by 1986, but still the numbers of cattle were down by four per cent.[6]

The standard of lamb and beef produced in Scotland is carefully monitored by a Quality Assurance Scheme operated by the Guild of Quality Scotch Meat Suppliers for its members. Disciplines are imposed at each stage of the production and marketing process, beginning with regular plant and product inspections. Strict rules governing the slaughter, handling, transport and retailing of the

A Dundee butcher's shop. Scotland has a reputation for quality meat.

(Scottish Tourist Board)

*The Scots' preference for beef is
well known.*

(Carter Rae)

meat are enforced, and only certain carcases defined in terms of levels of finish
and shape are eligible for inclusion. The
promotion of Scotch beef and lamb, both
in the UK and abroad, is handled by the
Scotch Quality Beef and Lamb Association Ltd, who aim to develop new
markets.

Although the Scots prefer beef, the
traditional Scottish butcher's shop is
changing. The white trays filled with
chops, mince and stewing steak are, with
changing eating habits, complemented by
what the MLC calls 'Kitchen Ready
Products' and a range of well trimmed
boneless cuts. 'We have to get more meat
into convenience foods' says Mr Donaldson, 'but not necessarily frozen foods; we
need a wider range of fresh meat cuts and
ready meal products to provide choice
and variety.' Thus the butcher shop that
once catered to the thrifty housewife, who
would boil a sheep's head for broth or
pig's trotters for potted meat, now displays meat kebabs, beef croquettes, lamb
burgers, stir fries and quick-fry coated
pork loin.

Aberdeen Angus is not the only breed
associated with quality beef: Scottish
herds also include Galloway, Highland
and Shorthorn, and, more recently, Continental imports like Charolais, Simmental and Limousin. One man who prefers
an Aberdeen Angus cross (preferably with
the Blue Grey), is Clive Davidson, prop-
rietor of Scotland's most acclaimed steak
house, Champany Inn, near Linlithgow.
Champany's cook their meat only by
charcoaling, and for this reason, the beef
they use must conform to a certain texture: 'the fat must be flakey and not
rubbery and there must be a certain
amount of marbling throughout the meat
to make it juicy,' says Mr Davidson.
'English grown beef is too rich in terms of
marbling and the Continental breeds like
Charolais and Simmental are too fibrous.'

To make certain he gets the kind of
beef he requires, Mr Davidson, a former
butcher, oversees the finishing of the beef
he will use. All of his animals are produced in Scotland and finished off for at
least five weeks on grain: too much grass,
he believes, gives the beef a bitter taste.
None of the meat he uses is ever frozen
but it is hung for a minimum of 21 days 'to
enhance flavour and give tenderness'. He
has even successfully experimented with
hanging meat for eight weeks. 'If the
colour of the meat is too deep red, like the
meat you buy in supermarkets,' he says,
'that means it is too fresh. The meat must

have a blue tinge.'

Mr Davidson's care with the feeding, butchering and hanging of meat has paid off as far as his restaurant trade is concerned. His nomination by the *Good Food Guide* as the 'best steak house in Britain', followed by an article in *The New York Sunday Times*, has ensured a steady stream of customers to his door – most of them from abroad.

Champany's use only prime cuts of beef: popeseye, sirloin, rib-eye and fillet. Lamb, which also figures on his menus, is butchered in the same way as the beef to provide fillet of lamb and lamb steak. Sirloin of lamb and rib-eye of lamb are described in the menu as being 'served pink only', an interesting requisite in view of the Scots preference for meat being 'well done'. 'Scots are meat eaters but they need to be educated to eat steak less well cooked,' says Mr Davidson. 'Steak should be served rare to medium rare – it breaks my heart when I am asked to cook a

steak well done.'

Poultry

The tough barnyard hen that has passed its laying days and can only be usefully boiled for traditional Cock-a-Leekie soup, has almost passed into history. Except for a few hens kept scratching on smallholdings – more as pets than for eggs and meat – chickens raised in Scotland today are more tender, and have more meat than ever before. 'When I first started in the poultry business 30 years ago,' says David Roberts, an independent poultry consultant, 'we could grow a 4lb. [1·8kg.] chicken in 12 weeks: now we can grow a 4lb. chicken in half that time. The efficiency and improvement in nutrition, processing and disease control is unbelievable.'

Poultry rearing is a thriving industry in Scotland today, unlike past centuries when the few chickens and geese kept by

Shetland lamb is regarded as a delicacy.

(Carter Rae)

49

farmers' tenants lived on scraps and were frequently used to pay the rent. Geese were often more common than hens, their feathers being considered valuable: in the eighteenth century geese in Orkney were even an exportable commodity. Only two genuine Scottish breeds of chicken survive today – the black Scots Dumpy, considered to be an ideal 'sitter' and the Scots Grey, a black and white non-sitting breed with a 200-year-old pedigree. Both of these breeds figure more prominently as show birds than in today's highly industrialised poultry rearing business. 'In the old days,' says Mr Roberts, 'there used to be a dual purpose bird like the Rhode Island Red or the Sussex Leghorn, a chicken used for both meat and eggs.' Nowadays, the emphasis is on the meat chicken and Scotland is one of the foremost international breeders of this type of poultry, thanks to the efforts of companies like Ross Breeders and Marshalls of Newbridge – the latter produce a roasting chicken up to 3·6kg (8lb.) in weight.

Modern poultry husbandry was introduced at the end of World War II from the US. Much of the Scottish success story can be traced to the work of the Poultry Research Centre (PRC), first established in 1947. The Centre is now located in Roslin, a village south of Edinburgh and it features modern, purpose-built laboratories, offices, poultry housing and a feed mill situated on a 5·7-hectare (14-acre) site. PRC is the main non-disease poultry research facility in the UK and its objective of improving the biological efficiency of poultry production has led to research in nutrition, environment, behaviour, genetics, metabolism and physiology.

The fresh chicken purchased by today's Scottish housewife has benefited from this research and from improved nutrition. A diet which once consisted of scraps and the odd handful of grain is now carefully controlled with appropriate amounts of wheat, soya bean, fish meal, a small amount of fat or oil for energy, maize, minerals and vitamins. Cereals account for over 75 per cent of the chicken's intake and these can be manipulated to change the colour of the chicken's flesh. The American preference for a yellow chicken – one that has been fed primarily on maize (with or without the addition of carotine for colouring – is in contrast to the British choice of a white chicken. In David Roberts' opinion, 'there is no discernible distinction between a bird fed to be yellow and a bird fed to be white, unless it is truly free range, twice the age and grown and matured like the "Label Rouge" and Loire chickens grown in France.' Yellow chickens, he says, are a 'marketing ploy'.

The very best quality chicken, he asserts, is a fresh chicken which has been killed three to five days before it gets to the customer. 'I look for a bird that has a big breast and thighs, one that is dry and has been cleanly plucked and processed, and well packaged and finished because someone has taken care with it.'

This description of a quality chicken fits the standards and products found in many of the large retail chain-stores. For Scottish cooks, it is a sharp contrast to the poultry that their ancestors used in both Cock-a-Leekie soup and chicken stovies. It means that we have no choice but to consign some of the old recipes to our collective memory.

1. 'Burns grace at Kirkcudbright' in *Robert Burns*, Langsyne Publishers, Newtongrange, 1984 (an edited facsimile of the Virtue edition of 1841).
2. *The Statistical Account of Scotland, 1791–99*, ed. Sir John Sinclair, Vol. XIV, Kincardine & South & West Aberdeenshire, E.P. Publishing, Wakefield 1982, p. 152.
3. *Ibid*, p. 154.
4. T. Bedford Franklin, *A History of Scottish Farming*, Thomas Nelson, Edinburgh 1952, p. 130.
5. Alexander Ramsay, *History of the Highland and Agricultural Society of Scotland*, William Blackwood & Sons, Edinburgh 1879, p. 198.
6. *Economic Report on Scottish Agriculture 1986*, Department of Agriculture and Fisheries for Scotland, Scottish Office 1987, p. 47.

Opposite: Musselburgh Pie.
(Victor Albrow)

Musselburgh Pie – a Modern Interpretation

Of all the traditional Scottish recipes, Musselburgh Pie is one of the most interesting and adaptable. The original is good enough but for a very special occasion – or for very special friends – the curious affinity of beef to shellfish can be exploited in various ways. Here are two very stylish recipes to take Musselburgh Pie into the next century. Perhaps we should call them Portobello Pie and Joppa Bridie respectively.

Portobello Pie – Fillet of Beef with Oysters in Puff Pastry

For 6:

900g. (2lb.) fillet of beef
6 large oysters
1 carrot
1 stick celery
1 medium onion
bay leaf, fresh thyme or tarragon
coarsely ground black peppercorns
50g. (2 oz.) butter
1 glass red wine
2 15ml. spoons (2 tablespoons) wine vinegar
home-made puff pastry (p. 102)

Trim a few scraps of meat and fat from the underside of the fillet. Fry them in butter in a heavy casserole with the vegetables, roughly chopped, until well browned.

Pour in the wine vinegar and boil to nothing until the liquid has disappeared. Pour in the wine. Add the herbs and a few peppercorns and a cup of cold water. Simmer for 1–2 hours, allowing the sauce to reduce to ⅓ of its volume. Strain and reserve.

Fry the beef in butter, seasoned only with crushed peppercorns, until well sealed. Roast for 10 minutes in a hot oven. Allow to cool.

Open the oysters, pour the liquor from each into the stock, and refrigerate the oysters until needed.

Roll out the puff pastry to a size easily big enough to hold the beef.

Make a lengthwise slit in the side of the beef, sparing the ends, and insert the oysters with a little chilled butter and chopped herbs.

Wrap the beef in pastry, sealing the edges well, and brush with beaten egg.

Bake in a hot oven (Gas 7, 475°F, 220°C) for 20–25 minutes when the pastry should be well risen and browned.

Meanwhile heat the sauce to simmering point. Off the heat, beat in the rest of the butter in small nuggets until the sauce is smooth and shiny.

Serve the beef in thick slices, with the sauce at the side. A crisp green vegetable such as stir-fried broccoli, or buttered fresh garden peas, would be an ideal accompaniment.

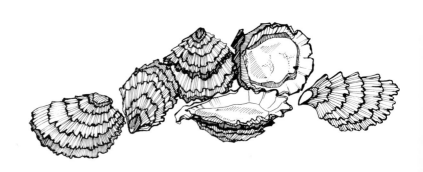

Joppa Bridies – Slices of Beef with Oysters in Individual Puff Pastry

This is an economical version of the above. In some ways it is closer to the original, and is both more economical and closer to the original if made with mussels. Allow 2 mussels in place of 1 oyster.

Prepare the stock as indicated above.

Cut the beef into 12 even slices

Open the oysters. Pour the liquor over the beef slices, and season with black pepper.

Wrap each oyster in a slice of beef

Roll out the pastry, and cut into 12 individual shapes. On each base place two oysters in their beef wrapping, and cover with a complementary shape. Seal well, brush with beaten egg and bake for 25 minutes in a hot oven.

Finish the sauce and serve with the individual pasties, with vegetables as suggested in the preceding recipe.

For 6:

450g. (1lb.) fillet of beef
1 dozen oysters
ingredients otherwise as above

Beef Stew with Beer and Dumplings

Suet dumplings, or doughballs, have long been popular as a savoury and nourishing accompaniment to a rich beef stew, though there is little tradition for stewing or braising meat. This same method can be used for oxtail, in which case red wine is better than beer.

Cut the beef into 5-cm. (2-inch) pieces. Coat with seasoned flour and brown in the butter.

Add the vegetables, roughly chopped, then the beer. Bring to the boil, add the garlic cloves and bouquet garni, and simmer for 2 hours or until the beef is tender.

Mix the ingredients of the dumplings with enough water to form a thick dough, and form them into 3·5 cm. (1½-inch) balls. Put these on top of the stew and cook for a further 20 minutes. Baked or roast potatoes and buttered peas complete a wholesome dish.

For 6:

900g. (2lb.) rump or round steak
600ml. (1 pint) pale ale
225g. (½lb.) carrots
2 sticks celery
4 medium onions, stuck with cloves
few garlic cloves
25g. (1 oz.) butter
25g. (1 oz.) flour
bouquet garni
salt, pepper

For the dumplings:

100g. (4 oz.) self-raising flour
50g. (2 oz.) suet
parsley and chives, chopped fine
salt

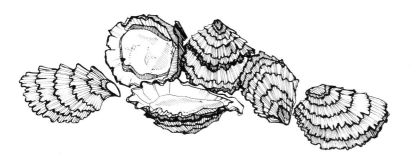

Fillet of Beef with a Red Wine and Shallot Sauce

Fillet of beef has had a bad press in recent years. The conventional wisdom is that it is flavourless and overpriced. This may be the case where the beef is of inferior quality or is insufficiently hung, but the fillet of Scottish beef is exquisitely succulent and tasty. Its fine texture takes a refined sauce, such as this modernised version of the old Bordeaux favourite. A gesture of thanks to the Auld Alliance and an acknowledgment of our traditional love of claret.

For 6:

675–900g. (1½–2lb.) beef fillet, in the piece
1 carrot
1 leek
1 onion
1 stick of celery
300ml. (½ pint) red wine
1 clove garlic
3 or 4 shallots
olive oil, lemon juice, fresh thyme
salt, coarsely ground black pepper
50g. (2 oz.) butter

At least 2 hours before the meal, trim all loose scraps from the underside of the fillet, with any adherent fat. Fry these in a little butter until brown, then add the chopped carrot, leek, celery and onion and allow these to brown. Pour in the red wine, add the garlic clove, chopped, and some fresh thyme. Simmer for 2 hours, allowing the liquid to reduce by about a half. Strain, season and reserve this stock.

Meanwhile marinate the fillet in olive oil, lemon juice and black pepper.

Brown the beef over a high heat in a heavy frying pan which can transfer to the oven. Roast in a high oven (Gas 7, 425°F, 220°C) for 20–25 minutes, then allow it to rest in a warm place while you finish the sauce.

In the pan used for the beef fry the shallots, very finely chopped, in butter until soft. Pour in a little red wine, and reduce this to nothing. Strain in the stock, bring to simmering point and then, away from the heat, swirl in enough small nuggets of butter as necessary to bring the sauce together. It should be fairly liquid, opaque but shiny.

Slice the beef, salt it lightly and arrange on warm plates with the sauce around it. Choose a single interesting vegetable as accompaniment, such as fresh garden peas.

Roast Leg of Lamb with Wild Thyme

Mutton no longer exists, denying us the hearty stews and Scotch broth of the past. Fortunately, the quality of Scottish lamb is excellent. If you are lucky you may even be able to buy a leg of Shetland lamb in autumn. These are a special breed, raised on the salty pastures of the seashore. They are therefore comparable with the famous *pré-salé* lambs of north-west France.

Lamb has an extraordinary affinity for olive oil, lemons, garlic and the stronger herbs. I prefer thyme to rosemary, and in summer wild thyme is easily found on the cliffs of the shoreline all round Scotland. Marinate a leg of lamb in oil, lemon juice and thyme, with a little crushed garlic and black pepper, for 24 hours if possible.

The secret in roasting lamb is to do it quickly in a high oven, in order to seal in the juices, and then to let it rest in a cool oven with the door ajar for up to an hour. It will then be evenly pink. For a 2·5–3-kg. (5–7-lb.) leg the initial roasting should be at Gas 8, 450°F, 230°C for 1–1½ hours. The last 20 minutes or so can be done on a spit, over a wood fire or barbecue, giving an exquisite flavour. After the obligatory rest period, carve the lamb and salt it lightly. Serve it with the gratin of potatoes and shallots (p. 72), and either the carrots with tarragon (p. 73) or fresh garden peas with mint and butter.

Lambs' Kidneys in Mustard Sauce

The Scots may not have been great meat-eaters in times gone by, presumably mainly for financial reasons, but for precisely those reasons we have always been fond of offal and off-cuts such as beef flank (boiled in stew) or oxtail. The high point of Scottish offal cookery is, of course, the haggis, still a firm everyday favourite throughout the land. Haggis apart, though, we have no tradition of fine recipes for offal. The extraordinarily high quality of Scottish lamb demands that it should be treated delicately to get the best out of it. These kidneys in mustard are best served in a puff pastry case with a plain green vegetable such as asparagus or green beans.

Remove any fat and membranes from the kidneys and put them to soak in cold water for 20 minutes or so.

Chop the onion and soften it in butter over a modest heat in a heavy saucepan, with the garlic clove, chopped fine, and a few slivers of boiled ham. Pour in the white wine and boil for a minute or two. Add the tomatoes, chopped roughly, the herbs and seasoning. Simmer for 20 minutes.

Dry the kidneys, season them and fry them gently in butter for about 2 minutes each side. They should feel resistant to the touch, and be evenly pink inside.

Beat the cream and egg yolks together, then beat in a ladleful of the just simmering sauce. Return this mixture to the saucepan, stirring constantly over a very low heat until the sauce just thickens. Remove it immediately from the heat and stir in 2 15ml. spoons (tablespoons) of fine prepared mustard. Taste for seasoning and add more mustard if necessary.

Slice the kidneys and serve on a bed of sauce, sprinkled with fresh chopped chives.

For 6:

12 lambs' kidneys
25g. (1 oz.) butter
1 onion
3–4 tomatoes
25g. (1 oz.) boiled ham
1 clove garlic
2 glasses white wine
150ml. (¼ pint) double cream
2 egg yolks
2 15ml. spoons (2 tablespoons) prepared mustard
bay leaf, fresh thyme or oregano, chives
salt, black pepper

Roast Fillet of Lamb with Spring Vegetables

Since lack of mutton forces us to use tender young lamb, there is no real point in cooking old-fashioned dishes of boiled mutton. The one stew which is still worth doing is Hotch Potch, a close relative of the French *navarin printannier*, in which the best end of neck is stewed with tomatoes and tender spring vegetables such as peas, green beans, white turnips and new potatoes. Here is a refinement of that dish which produces a succulent modern version of an age-old favourite.

For 6:

900g–1kg. (2–2½lb.) single loin of lamb, in
   the piece
225g. (½lb.) young carrots
2 sticks of celery
1 onion
450g. (1lb.) white turnips
450g. (1lb.) tomatoes
4–6 cloves of garlic
olive oil
lemon juice
1 15ml. (1 tablespoon) wine vinegar
1 glass red wine
salt and black pepper
fresh thyme

Remove the meat from the bone, and free it from all fat. Set it to marinate for a few hours in a mixture of olive oil, lemon juice, a little chopped garlic, thyme and black pepper.

Chop up the bones, and brown them well in a little oil in a heavy casserole with a carrot, the celery, and the onion, all roughly chopped. Add the vinegar and boil down. Pour in the red wine, top up with water (about 200ml. or ⅓ pint), add the tomatoes, chopped and seeded, the garlic, a few peppercorns and some fresh thyme. Simmer for 2–3 hours. Strain and reserve at least 2 hours before the meal, in order to allow the fat to separate.

About an hour before the meal, degrease the stock and bring it to simmering point in the casserole. Add the fresh vegetables in sequence so that they will all be tender but not overcooked at the time of serving.

As soon as the vegetables are tender, thicken the sauce with a little cornflour and set it aside.

Immediately before going to table, brown the 'fillet' in a little extra oil in a heavy ovenproof frying pan. Set it to roast for 10–15 minutes in a hot oven (Gas 7, 425°F, 220°C). If you prefer to have this done before going to table, put it to keep warm covered with foil.

Bring the sauce back to simmering point and swirl in a little butter. Serve on individual plates or on a platter, the meat carved into 1·25-cm. (½-inch) thick diagonally-cut slices, laid on top of the sauce and surrounded by vegetables.

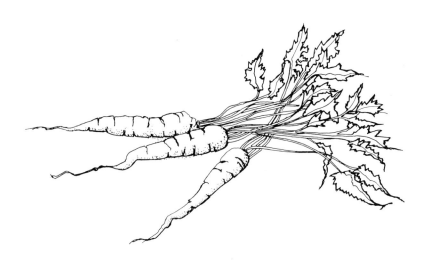

Chicken Howtowdie

Now that well flavoured chickens are becoming available once more this ancient recipe is worth reviving. The bird should ideally be both free range and corn fed. The word howtowdie is said to come from an old French word for a young hen *hutaudeau*. This is interesting, since traditionally boiling would have been the preferred method for cooking older birds. This, however, is a somewhat luxurious dish bearing comparison, for instance, with the Lyonnaise *poulet en demi-deuil*.

The chicken may be stuffed with a traditional sage and onion stuffing, or with skirlie (oatmeal fried in butter with onions).

Put the bird in a heavy casserole with 50g. (2 oz.) butter, the onions and the herbs. Turn the chicken in the butter over a medium heat until it begins to take colour.

Add the stock, season if necessary, and cook covered over a low heat for an hour, or until the chicken is tender.

Wash and chop the spinach, and cook it in butter until well reduced. Let it absorb plenty of butter. Season with a little salt, black pepper and nutmeg.

Meanwhile reduce the rest of the stock by half its volume to make a gravy. In it poach the eggs, and the chicken liver for a minute or so only.

Carve the chicken, and serve with the eggs in spinach 'nests'. Sieve the liver into the stock and gravy mix, stir to thicken and pour over the chicken.

For 6:

1 chicken
225g. (½lb.) pickling onions
225g. (½lb.) spinach
600ml. (1 pint) chicken stock
100g. (4 oz.) butter
6 eggs
fresh herbs (tarragon, chives, chervil, parsley)

Pot-Roast Chicken With Wild Mushrooms

If the forcemeat, liver and poached eggs of the traditional howtowdie seem too much, here is a modern treatment of the same theme based on a classic French method. Although no liquid is added a lovely concentrated sauce appears, as if by magic. Chanterelles are ideal, whether fresh or bottled, but if no wild mushrooms are available use cultivated or Paris mushrooms.

For 6:

1 chicken, trussed
1 medium onion
1 stick celery
1 large carrot
100g. (¹/₄lb.) mushrooms
1 clove garlic
50g. (2 oz.) butter
150ml. (¹/₄ pint) double cream
fresh tarragon, chervil or parsley

Season the bird inside and out, and insert the garlic clove, a sprig of tarragon and a knob of butter into the cavity.

Chop the vegetables and mushrooms roughly.

Brown the bird in butter in a cast-iron casserole. This is best done over a modest heat, turning the bird constantly for about 15 minutes.

Remove the bird. Wipe the casserole with kitchen paper to remove the browned butter. Add the remaining 25g. (1 oz.) of butter with the vegetables and mushrooms. Turn them over a moderate heat until they are well coated with butter.

Put a sprig of tarragon among the vegetables. Place the chicken on top, breast side down. Cover with a close fitting lid.

Place in a moderate oven, Gas 5, 375°F, 190°C, for 1 hour. The chicken should be tender but not falling apart.

Remove the chicken allowing the juices to run back into the casserole. Carve it and serve on a heated platter.

Remove any excess fat from the liquid in the casserole. Add the cream and boil down to a smooth consistency. Pour the sauce over the chicken, and sprinkle with chopped tarragon.

For a more elegant presentation, remove all of the vegetables from the sauce before adding the cream. Be sure not to remove the chanterelles.

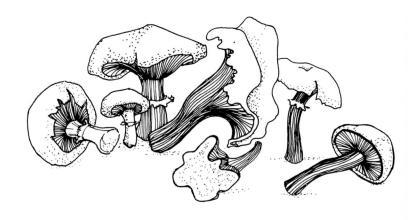

4. Vegetables & Fruit-Suited to Climate

Seed-potatoes, staring their eyes
out into the black, to sprout
as tentacles, bulge nodes.

Fat swedes that heave and shoulder
up the soil, cracking woody-
purplish, bursting for air.

Parsnips, one great tap-root
plunging its tip
to strike the centre of the earth

Beetroot, carrots, neeps, celeriac
– brute root-crops, vegetable,
shaping flesh, juicing
raw the blackness that begets us
gets us all.[1]

Scotland has a poor reputation when it comes to eating vegetables. Root crops like turnips, potatoes and carrots have tended to dominate traditional cookery, although kale, a rich source of Vitamin C, was once eaten extensively by the poorer classes. Before potatoes were introduced in Orkney and Shetland in the mid-eighteenth century, kale was the vegetable eaten to combat scurvy. Scurvy – a disease marked by bleeding of the gums due to lack of Vitamin C – was all too prevalent in a diet which relied heavily on salt fish.

Kale was often sown in August on common grazing land and then transplanted in the spring to enclosed gardens by dwelling-houses. These 'kailyards', which were common to other parts of the country as well, were an important asset since kale and cabbage were also used to feed livestock. Kale was the primary ingredient in broth and simple supper dishes. The Northern Islanders boiled it together with 'knocked corn' (a type of barley) or potatoes. Another popular method of preparing kale, was to boil it and thicken it with oatmeal.

Nowadays, kale is more often grown for cattle feed than to grace a table – yet its nutritional value remains unchanged. Curly kale, which can be grown in any garden, overwinters well and its young spring leaves can be eaten raw with a complementary salad dressing. The outer leaves require cooking and are a tasty addition to traditional broths. (See recipe for pheasant braised with curly kale, p. 39)

Poor circumstances dictated the reliance on kale and potatoes in years past. In the late seventeenth century, however, it is established that the gentry, at least, had access to a much more imaginative diet. *The Scots Gard'ner*, first published in 1683, contained instructions for planting a wide variety of vegetables including spinach, sorrel, celery, chicory and endive, garlic, shallots, cucumber, onions, leeks and parsnips as well as a number of herbs. Written by John Reid, son and grandson of gardeners at Niddry Castle in Edinburgh, the book in its many versions was destined to become a basic manual for years to come. It dealt not only with suggestions about planting but directions for laying out gardens and to some extent for cooking:

You may love leeks with a cock. Onions may be baked with a little butter if you want meat . . . boil collyflowers in water mixed with a little milk; then pour it off, and mix them in a stew-pan with sweet-butter seasoned with salt, and so serve them up about boiled mutton . . . Boil cabbage with beef . . . Boil and peel parsnips, chop and bruise them well, pour on butter, and set them on a coal, and if you please strew a little cinnamon upon them . . .[2]

A Scottish ship's surgeon, James Lind, was the first to prescribe fruit and vegetables as a cure for scurvy. The practice quickly spread: history records that in 1781 two fleets were anchored at Leith for seven weeks and several thousand sailors suffering from scurvy were given a daily supply of fresh vegetables.

By the early nineteenth century, the city populace at least had access to quite a variety of vegetables through the markets in Glasgow and Edinburgh. In addition to

Previous page: Raspberries in abundance.

(Della Matheson)

60

the root vegetables, cabbage and kale, there was celery, cauliflower, broccoli, peas, beans and asparagus, savoys, onions, and leeks.

Today the availability of vegetables in Scotland is even wider thanks to the influence of Asian immigrants, emphasis on the use of dried pulses in both salad and vegetarian dishes, and changing cooking habits: stir-fried vegetables which can be bought either fresh or frozen for the wok have expanded the repertoire of many cooks. Many of these vegetables, however, are imported and not grown in Scotland.

In 1986 the amount of land in Scotland given over to growing vegetables for human consumption, was 3·1 thousand hectares (7·6 thousand acres). An additional 12·2 thousand (30·6 thousand acres) were used for growing potatoes and a further 17·2 thousand hectares (43 thousand

acres) for seed potatoes.[3] Potatoes are certainly one of Scotland's most successful vegetables. The climatic conditions of the country are particularly suited to the cultivation of this historically significant tuber (principal production areas are in Fife and Tayside), and Scotland has a well-deserved reputation for both potato research and for export: it is the predominant supplier of seed potatoes to England and Wales and in years past has also sent quantities of seed potatoes to the Mediterranean countries. Yet for all this success in export, there are problems in the Scottish potato industry due to static consumption but increased yield.

Potato breeding is the largest of the breeding departments of the Scottish Crop Research Institute, which is funded by the Department of Agriculture and Fisheries. And, in addition to developing new varieties, the SCRI has also worked

Planting seed potatoes in East Lothian.

(National Museums of Scotland)

Organic vegetables grown in Perthshire by Ken Paterson.
(Della Matheson)

with organic vegetable growers in an attempt to find varieties which might be less susceptible to blight – one of the inevitable risks in growing without use of chemicals. Scotland's fledgling organic producers are still very much in the business of trying to educate the public about the advantages of their products and to solving their marketing and promotional challenges. There are roughly 120 organic farmers in Scotland (many being smallholders) and a further 100 organic gardeners. The total area cropped, including forage but excluding hill land, is about 1000 hectares (2471 acres), or ·08 per cent of the total area of crops. Vegetables, potatoes and fruit account for more than half of this total.[4]

Ken Paterson, of 'Simply Organic' at Kinfauns by Perth, grows 22 different vegetables in his old-fashioned market garden, including such things as spinach, peppers, peas, kale and dwarf beans. He chooses and grows his varieties for their flavours. 'My vegetables have a sweet, delicate taste because of the way we grow them – at their normal rate rather than by force,' he says. He admits that organic growers expect a lower yield than farmers who use chemicals. 'Continuity and quality are two musts for organic growers,' he says. 'There must be a continuous supply of fresh produce.'

Another organic vegetable grower is Peter Erskine at Cambo Farm, one mile (1·5km.) south of Kingsbarns in the East Neuk of Fife. Cambo Farm has a number of attractions for the family, including a nature trail and a pet corner where children can see a wide range of Scottish farm animals. Their vegetable garden is also open to the public and organically grown cabbages can been seen in abundance. Other vegetables grown on the farm include potatoes, peas, carrots, summer cauliflower and 16·19 hectares (40 acres) of broccoli – 'a crop which grows very well in Scotland,' according to Mr Erskine. A lot of his produce, especially peas, goes for freezing and 'some years are better than others'.

The freezing of vegetables, rather than canning, has changed the nature of the industry over the past 15 years. 'The industry has moved from market gardening, supply the wholesale markets in Edinburgh and Glasgow, to an industry that is supplying processors or the major multiples through pre-packing,' said John Whitehead, chairman of both the NFU Scotland and the NFU Field Vegetable Committee. 'There is quite a dramatic expansion in vegetable growing in the Borders, Fife and Tayside but the number of people in growing has declined – fewer are growing more.'

Mr Whitehead is development manager for Scotfresh Ltd, a firm which freezes 20 320 tonnes (20 000 tons) of vegetables yearly. Peas, cauliflower, brussel sprouts, runner beans and broccoli are the vegetables most commonly frozen by the firm, but they also market mixed vegetable dishes in response to public demand for healthier eating. Scotfresh growers use 'module' plants for growing, plants that are first grown in trays and then transferred to the fields. Scotfresh have used the system (because it provides evenly maturing plants) since 1983, especially for crops such as sprouts, cauliflower, broccoli and leeks.

Broccoli is one vegetable, like potatoes, that is suited to the Scottish climate and Fife is one of the main growing areas of Europe. The production of leeks, a traditional Scottish vegetable, is also on the increase and some of the smaller producers are experimenting with vegetables such as mange tout and other rarities. One of these growers is Mrs Marlyn Whitehead who, like her husband, is also involved in vegetable growing. Her garden of three hectares (eight acres) in Fife, boasts celeriac, 'an old vegetable which used to be grown in walled gardens', red lettuce and romanesco, a cross between broccoli and cauliflower. Mrs Whitehead, who numbers several restaurants among her customers, quite often has to explain to people how to cook

her vegetables. 'Romanesco,' she declares, 'is the designer vegetable of the future. It is very yuppie and also very suited to the Scottish climate.'

While Fife may produce the ideal climate for broccoli and cauliflower, it is the Clyde Valley which has gained the reputation for salad ingredients, especially tomatoes. Clyde Valley growers have, of course, always depended on glass houses and in 1968, before oil prices increased, tomato production in the Valley, in 40·47 hectares (100 acres) of glass, was 3810 tonnes (3750 tons). By 1977, the area under glass had fallen to 20 hectares (50 acres) and production to 2032 tonnes (2000 tons) and in 1987, with the area

Cabbages growing at Cambo Farm in the East Neuk of Fife.
(Michael Siebert)

halved to 9·7 hectares (24 acres), production stood at 2540 tonnes (2500 tons).[5] The decrease in tomato production has, however, been compensated for by other types of planting. Flowers, trees and shrubs now account for some of the tomato shortfall. But food crops are also still in evidence – along with tomatoes, the Clyde Valley now boasts crops like lettuce, cyboes (spring onions), cucumbers, courgettes and squashes.

Seaweed

Cultivated vegetables, of course, require time and gardening expertise whereas one of the oldest and most healthy plants –

seaweed – could be gathered free. Soups made of freshly gathered seaweed were once quite popular in Orkney, Shetland and the Western Isles. Children often ate raw seaweed stalks or cooked it over a peat fire and put it on bannocks. The mineral salts, vitamins and high iodine content of these plants made them a particularly important component in a restricted diet.

Seaweed is still being harvested, but with the help of science. Julian Clokie, a marine biologist, decided to turn his hand to harvesting 'sea vegetables' about 1984 in order to realise 'some of the great potential' in the waters around Scotland. He works from an eighteenth-century farmhouse at Balmuchy, near Fearn in Ross-shire, where he has installed a drier to process the fresh seaweed after it is brought ashore. His partner, Hamish Mackenzie, handles most of the diving in the Moray Firth, and harvesting is done between the end of March and the middle of July.

Clokie's venture into harvesting and marketing seaweed as a food has taken a great deal of research. At present, he harvests seven different varieties including sugar and finger ware, dabberlocks, grockle, summer and autumn dulse and purple nori. Each of the vegetables has to be harvested when it is in its prime. The gathering is done from a rowboat, since any motorised boat would leave traces of petrol in the water which would affect the taste. The 'sharp, bright taste' he achieves, he says, 'can only be accomplished by critical harvesting and quick drying.' His drier can accommodate half a tonne of seaweed at a time but prior to being dried the seaweed must be carefully sorted by hand. The packaging into manageable weights (packets can be purchased by mail order in varying sizes and seaweed is also supplied loose) is also handled on site.

Clokie's main problem with The Sea Vegetable Company Ltd is not so much harvesting and drying as convincing the British public that seaweed is an enjoyable addition to many different types of dishes, whether meat based or vegetarian. Grockle, he says, has a flavour of roasted

Glass houses make possible the growing of more unusual vegetables.

(Della Matheson)

chestnuts, while purple nori is reminiscent of oyster liquor and sugar ware can be compared to winter cabbage, since it retains its crispness when fried and can be used in salads with sprouted vegetables.

Herbs are another of nature's resources and their propagation has a long and varied history. The forerunner of the Royal Botanic Garden in Edinburgh was a herbal or 'physick garden' first planted by a group of Edinburgh physicians in 1656. Using a piece of ground belonging to Holyroodhouse, they amassed over 900 plants – many from foreign countries. The herbs used by these physicians were of course for 'medicinal' purposes, not for flavouring food. In the past Scots have never been overly imaginative in the use of herbs for seasoning. Nowadays, the appreciation of herbs is more universal. Most cooks still rely on the dried variety but 'fresh herbs make a great difference to cooking and they all have very specific aromas,' said Stan Turner of Scotherbs in Perthshire. 'Herbs are all very positive in flavour and when you use them for the first time you need to use them in small quantities . . . you can always add a little more next time.' Scotherbs is located at Waterybutts, by Errol, in the Carse of Gowrie, and the public are welcome to browse through the 'Herbare' from mid-April to mid-October. They grow 85 types of cooking herbs and are happy to supply freshly harvested herbs or plants, as well as advising on the use of herbs in cooking.

'People can walk around our garden, pick leaves and test the herbs,' invited Mr Turner. 'All herbs rely on their oils to give off that smell and flavour. A herb like Lovage is so strong and distinctive that if you distil the oil from its leaves, you can still taste the flavour after it has been diluted.'

Soft Fruit in Abundance

Raspberries are perhaps the best known of the many soft fruits produced in Scotland and until the recent competition from Eastern Europe, growers in Tayside were producing 70 per cent of the raspberries sold on the Continent.

Certain areas of the country are particularly ideal for growing fruit: the Carse of Gowrie, between Perth and Dundee, with its rich soil, and relatively low rainfall, produces most of Scotland's raspberries and strawberries, although the fruits also grow well around the Moray Firth, and 'pick-your-own farms' can be found

Scottish raspberries are grown for consumption at home and abroad.

(Della Matheson)

in East Lothian and Perthshire.

The most popular variety of raspberry cultivated by growers is the Glen Clova – considered to be an ideal for jam, freezing and canning. It can be grown earlier than other varieties, which is another point in its favour. The soft fruit cultivated in Scotland, however, also includes black-currants and tayberries (a blackberry/raspberry hybrid). Such a hybrid also produced the Loganberry, first dis-covered in the 1880s, a fruit very popular in the South.

Fruit processing in Scotland nowadays is a major industry and the cultivation of soft fruit in the country is measured at over 2000 hectares (4942 acres). Re-search and the breeding of new varieties, to support the industry, is carried on in the soft fruit department of the Scottish Crop Research Institute in Dundee.

High labour costs have increased the number of pick-your-own farms, though in some areas the numbers of these farms

has dwindled. The Boggs in Pencaitland, East Lothian, a fertile growing area formerly owned by the Department of Agriculture, had at one time 42 holdings: now only three are given over to fruit. Couples like George and Elizabeth Auld, who retired recently after 36 years as strawberry growers, remember well the days before 'pick your own', when a steady stream of lorries used to arrive on site to take berries to the market. 'Twenty years ago we had as many as 50 school-children all picking berries in the fields during the summer,' recalled Mrs Auld. 'The first day we turned a blind eye and they ate as many strawberries as they wanted. After that, they didn't want to look at a strawberry!'

Pick your own is still a popular pastime with canny Scots cooks who like making jam or freezing berries and during the height of the season – July – strawberry growers like the Aulds, work from 6 am to 9 pm, although as both readily admit,

Opposite and above: The herb garden – popular throughout the centuries. The Scotherb garden near Errol, where the public is encouraged to browse.
(Della Matheson)

Pick your own soft fruit is now a favourite pastime, but a high percentage of fruit is still professionally picked.

(Della Matheson)

March and in May the rows of plants are rotovated. When the plants are in flower they have to be sprayed to protect them against strawberry weevil and in June, straw has to be put under the plants to prevent the fruit rotting on the ground. Weeding is a continuous operation – as soon as the end of one field is reached, it is necessary to go back and start again.

Market gardens, once called 'Mail' gardens because their produce was carried to Glasgow and Edinburgh, have provided soft fruit to the Scottish populace for well over 200 years. Vegetables were being supplied to the citizens of Edinburgh by market gardeners from about the mid-1700s and in 1810, the populace of the capital was recorded as having consumed 28415 litres (50000 pints) of gooseberries, 17049 litres (30000 pints) of red and whitecurrants, and 1137 litres (2000 pints) of blackcurrants. However, only 568 litres (1000 pints) of raspberries were sold[6] – the popularity of this fruit did not grow until the present century.

Strawberries, a popular fruit with the Victorians, were grown in abundance in the Clyde Valley at the beginning of this century as were Victoria Plums. One has to look longingly back in time, however, to get a complete picture of the country's fruit-growing capabilities. Fruit trees, which were brought to Scotland in medieval times by the monks for the abbey gardens, once proliferated. Now plums, apples, cherries and pears are more likely to be harvested from private gardens than commercial orchards. The growing of melons is also a centuries-old practice: John Reid took special pains to describe the construction of hot beds for just this fruit – trenches ·6 metres (two feet) deep filled with 'dung and litter from the stables', topped with 'four inches (108mm) of rich, fresh and clean sifted mould'.[7]

Rhubarb, now cooked and used as a fruit, has always grown well in the Scottish climate, its properties once being considered medicinal, while apricots and peaches have also thrived – if not in abundance then at least with the help of

being soft fruit farmers is a year-round occupation. When they worked Orchardfield in The Boggs Holdings, they regularly planted 24000 new strawberry plants each April and May. New strawberry plants take a year to produce, and at the end of two years of fruiting, the plants are lifted and a crop of barley or some other grain is sown. 'We used to have about two acres (·809 hectares) with young strawberries, two with mature plants and two under crop,' explained Mr Auld.

The quality of each year's strawberry crop not only depends on the elements – a wet summer can totally destroy the crop – but on backbreaking care. Weeding and fertilising of the strawberries starts in south-facing walls. 'The only fruits for this country are apples, pears, cherries, plumbs, and apricocks, and peaches at south-walls, currants, gooseberries, raspberries etc.,'[8] wrote Reid. Almost any fruit – with the general exception of tropical varieties (pineapples aside, for these, too, were once grown in Scotland in special pits) – could be grown in Scotland in Reid's opinion. Regrettably, his enthusiasm for the cultivation of these many different fruits has not lasted, although a latter-day pioneer may be found in Robert Irvine, who has developed an astonishing Hydroponicum at Achiltibuie, north of Ullapool.

Hydroponic (water) culture is as old as the Hanging Gardens of Babylon, but was virtually unheard of in Scotland when Irvine started his venture. The effects of abandoning cold soil in favour of a trickle feed of water plus a nutrient, with the aid only of a triple-glazed polycarbonate roof, is startling. Irvine crops his first strawberries in April, his last in November. 'I have a motto – get off the ground and the sky is your limit!' He grows six varieties of figs, and plants grow so quickly that he will get three crops of courgettes in a season, while mange tout peas grow from seedlings to the roof in eight weeks flat. It is a brave and exciting venture in the windy and barren Highlands.

1. 'Root-crops' by Derek Bowman in *Made in Scotland* (ed. Robert Garioch), Carcanet Press, Chatham 1974, p. 65.
2. John Reid, *The Scots Gardener for the Climate of Scotland* (enlarged edition), Leith 1766, p. 137.
3. *Agricultural Statistics* (Scotland), HMSO, June 1987.
4. Peggy L. Dixon and John C. Holmes, *Organic Farming in Scotland*. The Edinburgh School of Agriculture in association with the Scottish International Education Trust, May 1987, p. ii.
5. John Leese, 'The Salad Bowl', *Scottish Food Trade Journal*, February 1988.
6. E. H. M. Cox, *A History of Gardening in Scotland*, Chatto & Windus, London 1935, p. 178.
7. John Reid, *op. cit.* p. 8.
8. *Ibid.*, p. 99.

Rich soil and a low rainfall make the Carse of Gowrie a productive area for soft fruit.
(Della Matheson)

Leek and Potato Gratin

The relative proportions of the ingredients in this recipe are unimportant. What matters is that it should be rich and creamy, with an enticing golden crust. It is a perfect accompaniment to a plain roast, or any meat served with a brown sauce.

Boil 3 or 4 of the potatoes in their skins and allow them to cool. This can be done well in advance, or even better, use leftover potatoes (e.g., cold gratin dauphinois)

Peel the remaining potatoes and boil them in salted water until soft. Mash them thoroughly with 50g. (2 oz.) butter, some of the cream and enough milk to make a moist, creamy purée.

Split the leeks lengthwise, and wash thoroughly. Chop them roughly and sweat in half of the butter with chopped onions and garlic.

When the leeks are soft and reduced (about 10 minutes), pour in most of the cream, and the herbs, and simmer for 5 minutes.

Put the leeks in the bottom of an ashet (a large meat dish, from the French: *assiette*), cover with the mashed potatoes, then, finally, with the cold potatoes cut into thick slices. Brush the surface with butter, season with black pepper, and bake in a moderate oven for 1 hour. Finish in the top of a hot oven if the surface is insufficiently browned.

For 6–8 people:

450–900g. (1–2lb.) potatoes
450g. (1lb.) leeks
1 medium onion
2 cloves garlic
mixed fresh herbs (parsley, chives, tarragon or chervil)
75–100g. (3–4 oz.) butter
200ml. (about ⅓ pint) double cream

Stovies

Stoved potatoes – reputedly so-called from the French *étuve* (a closed vessel) – exemplify peasant food at its best. At its simplest, roughly chopped potatoes are cooked for a long time in a closed vessel with a little butter or dripping, water and seasoning. This ends up as a delicious mess, but it can also function as a vehicle for something more ambitious. The first variation is to add onion, fried in beef dripping, the second to add layers of chicken. Most interesting is the dish of stoved tatties with limpets from the Western Isles, the courage and energy for which I have so far lacked. The chicken version would be good (using sliced rather than chopped potatoes in alternating layers with chicken pieces in butter and onion), especially if wild mushrooms were included. I find the following compromise most useful, providing a rich and savoury accompaniment to almost any highly flavoured meat or poultry dish. It is a return to the French method – most appropriate, in the circumstances.

Leek and Potato Gratin.

(Victor Albrow)

Gratin of Potatoes with Shallots and Wild Mushrooms

For 6:

900g. (2lb.) waxy potatoes (e.g. Desirée or
    Romano)
75g. (3 oz.) butter
150ml. (1 cup) good chicken stock
2 shallots or 1 small onion
450g. (1lb.) wild mushrooms (cèpes,
    chanterelles or field mushrooms) or 225g.
    (1/2lb) cultivated mushrooms and 1 small
    packet dried cèpes
1 clove garlic
salt and black pepper
parsley

Preheat the oven to Gas 4, 350°F, 180°C.

Peel and slice the potatoes 2mm. thick. A food processor makes light of this.

Slice the mushrooms (first soaking the dried cèpes, if necessary) and chop the shallots finely.

Fry the mushrooms in 25g. (1 oz.) of the butter over a high heat until they are reduced in size and all liquid is drawn off. And the shallot, reduce the heat and fry gently for a minute or two.

Butter a shallow ovenproof dish big enough to take the potatoes to a depth of around 5cm. (2 inches). Squeeze the garlic into the base of the dish, and cover with a layer of potatoes 2–3 slices deep. Season with salt and black pepper.

Add the mushrooms and shallots in a single layer. Season and sprinkle generously with chopped parsley.

Add the rest of the potatoes, seasoning every second or third layer.

Heat the stock and pour over the potatoes. Brush the surface with the rest of the butter, trying to cover every exposed slice of potato, and season with a final few turns of the pepper mill.

Place in the pre-heated oven for around 1½ hours. The crust should be golden brown.

NOTE: If roasting meat or fowl in a hot oven, the potatoes will cook happily underneath.

Beetroot Salad

Beetroot is a splendid vegetable, ideal as a partner for many of our best savoury dishes. This simple salad is good warm, for instance, with herring or trout fried in oatmeal and new potatoes, or cold with leftover beef or mutton. I prefer this version to any of those using mayonnaise or sour cream.

450g. (1lb.) boiled beetroot, hot or cold
1 5ml spoon (1 teaspoon) prepared mustard
olive oil
wine vinegar or lemon juice
black pepper
chives or flat-leaf parsley, finely chopped

Dice the beetroot roughly into a serving dish.

Make a vinaigrette with the mustard, olive oil and vinegar or lemon juice.

Dress the beetroot with the vinaigrette and herbs.

Clapshot

The combination of mashed potato and turnip is so obvious that we had been eating it for many years in our household, quite unaware of its ancient Orcadian provenance. Success depends on adequate quantities of butter and milk.

Peel the potatoes and turnips and chop them into manageable sizes, the turnip slightly smaller than the potato. Boil them with the garlic in heavily salted water until both vegetables are quite tender (the garlic will be soft and attenuated in flavour).

Drain the vegetables, being careful not to lose the garlic. Mash them thoroughly, adding butter and milk until you have a moist and creamy purée. Season with black pepper, and mix in the chopped chives.

Serve with stews such as the beef stew with beer and dumplings, or any hearty main course.

900g. (2lb.) potatoes
450g. (1lb.) turnips (swedes)
100g. (¼lb.) butter
125ml. (¼ pint) milk
2–6 cloves garlic, peeled
salt, black pepper
chives

Carrots in Tarragon and Egg Yolk Sauce

Here is an easy substitute for bearnaise sauce. The perfect accompaniment for roast or grilled lamb.

Peel and prepare the carrots. Simmer in lightly salted water until just tender.

Drain the carrots. Add the wine and butter and allow the alcohol to evaporate over a low heat for a minute or two.

Off the heat, add the lemon juice. Allow the carrots to cool slightly. Season with pepper.

Beat the egg yolks. Add them to the pan with the chopped tarragon and return it to the stove. Over a low heat, stir constantly until the sauce just thickens. Transfer carrots and sauce immediately to a warm (not hot) serving dish. The last stage needs careful attention or you will have a dish of scrambled egg with carrots.

For 6:

450g. (1lb.) young carrots
25g. (1 oz.) butter
2–3 egg yolks
½ glass white wine
juice of a lemon
salt and pepper
fresh tarragon

Shredded Brussels Sprouts Stir-Fried with Toasted Almonds

This method brings out a surprising delicacy in the flavour of the sprouts. It is perfect with game or beef.

Wash and dry the sprouts. Shred them by slicing rounds with a sharp knife.

Blanch and peel the almonds. Chop roughly and toast lightly on aluminium foil.

Heat a wok or large frying pan. Pour in the oil or butter/oil mixture. Add the sprouts and stir-fry over a moderate heat for a minute or two until they begin to wilt.

Stir the almonds into the sprouts with a dash of salt and pepper (very little seasoning is needed in stir-fries) and serve immediately.

For 6:

450g. (1lb.) brussels sprouts
25g. (1 oz.) whole almonds
hazelnut oil, olive oil or vegetable oil and
butter
salt and black pepper

Opposite: Raspberry Puffs with Cranachan and Blackcurrant Coulis.

(Victor Albrow)

Steamed Broccoli with Hazelnuts

Broccoli needs judicious cooking. When overcooked and soggy it is one of the worst of vegetables, but when undercooked and fibrous it can be equally unpleasant. The best results are obtained by cooking the stalks and the flowerheads for different lengths of time. Steaming is very effective, and need not be boring if the vegetables are immediately turned in butter, or, as in this recipe, an interesting vegetable oil.

This same method can be adapted for other vegetables. Green beans may be used in place of the broccoli, or courgettes can be dressed with olive oil and garnished with toasted pine kernels and raisins. A little mashed anchovy adds piquancy. Serve any of these recipes tepid as a starter, or use the simpler versions as an accompaniment to plain grilled fish.

For 6:

450g. (1lb.) broccoli
50g. (2 oz.) hazelnuts
30–45ml. (2–3 tablespoons) hazelnut oil
salt, black pepper

Wash the broccoli and divide just below the flowers. Peel the stalks, and steam them for 2 minutes. Add the flowers and steam for a further 2–3 minutes, until both are just tender.

Transfer immediately to a frying pan containing the oil, heated through but not smoking. Season to taste.

Toast the nuts, chop them roughly and sprinkle over the broccoli. Turn the broccoli gently in the oil, and serve on a warm dish.

Raspberry Puffs with Cranachan and Blackcurrant Coulis

Cranachan is an old harvest-time dish of many versions, ranging from a simple mixture of whipped cream, sugar and toasted oatmeal (with or without raspberries) to more elaborate confections including whisky and honey. Most authentic recipes contain fresh cream cheese, which in this recipe is used with lightly whipped cream to set off the glorious flavours of soft fruits in summer.

For 6:

12 individual puff pastries, shaped and baked
according to master recipe (p. 102)
150ml. (¼ pint) whipping cream
300ml. (½ pint) fresh cream cheese
50g. (2 oz.) medium oatmeal
small glass malt whisky
1 15ml. spoon (1 tablespoon) sugar
1 15ml. spoon (1 tablespoon) honey
225g. (½lb.) fresh raspberries
225g. (½lb.) blackcurrants
50g. (2 oz.) vanilla sugar (caster)

Soak the oatmeal in whisky with the honey for a few hours.

Whip the cream until it doubles in volume and fold it into the cream cheese.

Mix the oatmeal and whisky mixture into the cream and cream cheese.

Slice the tops off the pastry puffs. Fill the bottom half with a layer of cranachan. Cover with a layer of raspberries and a further layer of cranachan. Replace the tops and dust with icing sugar.

Purée the blackcurrants and sweeten to taste with the vanilla sugar. (A dash of red wine – preferably burgundy – can be added).

Serve on individual plates, garnished with whole blackcurrants or raspberries, and mint leaves.

Hazelnut Flan with Strawberries

This is a light, nutty cake, ideal for summer fruit.

For the pastry:

3 egg whites
125g. (5 oz.) caster sugar
75g. (3 oz.) hazelnuts
50g. (2 oz.) plain flour
25g. (1 oz.) melted butter

For the filling:

450g. (1lb.) fresh strawberries
150ml. (¼ pint) double or whipping cream
vanilla (caster) sugar
kirsch

Blend the nuts in a food processor until chopped very fine.

Whip the egg whites until stiff. Fold in the sugar, flour and nuts in turn, then the melted butter.

Spread the mixture in 2 17·5-cm. (seven-inch) cake tins and bake at Gas 4, 350°F, 180°C for 25–30 minutes, until they are evenly biscuit-coloured.

Wash the strawberries and sprinkle with vanilla sugar. Refrigerate ¾ of them. Press the remaining ¼ through a sieve to make a coulis, and moisten this with a little kirsch or a fruit-based eau-de-vie.

Spread one flan with whipped cream and arrange a layer of strawberries on top. Spread with a little more whipped cream, place the second flan on top and sprinkle with sugar.

Serve wedges of flan surrounded by the coulis, with a few whole strawberries.

Autumn Fruits in Claret Syrup

The archetypal autumn fruit of Scotland is the bramble, or blackberry. They are excellent in pies and crumbles, especially when mixed with apples, but are seldom served uncooked. In this recipe they are mixed with other fruits in a heavy, claret flavoured syrup. They can be served with choux pastry puffs or individual brioches stuffed with whipped cream.

Make a heavy syrup with the claret and sugar. Add the vanilla pod, a few slivers of lemon rind, a few brambles and a turn or two of black pepper, and simmer for 10 minutes to drive off some of the alcohol.

Allow the syrup to cool, then decant clear. Add the fruit (the apple chopped into 1·5-cm or ½-inch pieces) and adjust the sweetness if necessary. Pour in port to taste.

450g. (1lb.) mixed brambles, apples,
*   blackcurrants or other soft fruits.*
300ml. (½ pint) claret
small glass port
100g. (¼lb.) sugar (approx.)
lemon, peel, vanilla pod, clove, black pepper

Blaeberry Tart

This recipe is generic to all of the soft fruit tarts. Strawberries, raspberries, blackcurrants are all equally good, and redcurrants or wild (alpine) strawberries make a delightful addition to any of these. The essentials for success are a biscuity sweet shortcrust and a rich custard cream. Cultivated blueberries can be substituted for blaeberries (bilberries).

Beat the sugar gradually into the egg yolks and continue beating for a few minutes, until the mixture is pale and thickens slightly.

Slowly pour on the boiling milk, beating constantly.

Set this mixture over a moderate heat in a saucepan. Stir with a whisk until it boils. It will form lumps, but these disappear as you continue beating. Now beat over a low heat for 2 or 3 minutes.

Remove from the heat and beat in the butter, then the vanilla essence. The custard is now ready. If it is not to be used immediately, dot the surface with softened butter. (It may be kept in a refrigerator for a week.)

Make a glaze by boiling the jelly and sugar together with a little water until sticky.

Paint the base of the tart shell with the glaze and allow it to cool.

Spread a 1·5-cm (½-inch) layer of cold custard in the base of the tart. Distribute the fruit on top. Paint a coating of glaze over the fruit, and decorate with fresh mint leaves.

1 25-cm. (10-inch) fully baked pastry shell
*   (sweet shortcrust pastry, p. 104)*
450g. (1lb.) blaeberries
150ml. (1 cup) redcurrant jelly
2 15ml. spoons (2 tablespoons) sugar

For the custard cream:

150ml. (1 cup) sugar
5 egg yolks
⅔ cup flour (plain)
2 cups boiling milk
25g. (1 oz.) butter
1 15ml. spoon (1 tablespoon) vanilla extract

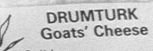

DRUMTURK GOATS
MRS DENISE FERGUSON
CORB, BRIDGE OF CALLY
BLAIRGOWRIE
PERTHSHIRE PH10 7JX
TEL. (025086) 267

DRUMTURK
Goats' Cheese

Sell by:

Ingredients: Goats milk, cream, salt,
bacterial culture, rennet, black pepper.

KEEP REFRIGERATED

5. Dairy Produce-Adapting to Change

. . . each farm had a fully matured cheese open for cooking and a softer one for eating. At breakfast, porridge was followed on alternate days by bacon and eggs or toasted cheese on a scone made of home-ground flour eaten in front of the fire.[1]

The tradition of cheesemaking in Scotland is a long one, with records of one cheese, Caboc, dating back to the fifteenth century in the Outer Isles. Most cattle were reared for meat rather than milk. Dairying was – and still is – concentrated in the fertile south-western areas, Ayrshire, Dumfries and Galloway.

For the most part, the normal cheese-making activity on the farm would have been restricted to 'crowdie', a skimmed milk cheese. Crowdie was quite simply made as a way of using up milk – and, of course, it had excellent nutritional value. (After the advent of the Milk Marketing Boards with their statutory obligation to buy all milk produced, the making of crowdie fell off, and few cheese producers now make it.)

The renowned nutty and golden Ayrshire Dunlop cheeses were first produced, so the story goes, by a woman called Barbara Gilmour, who learned the secret during a sojourn in Ireland. She had established her cheeses by 1688, and for most of the next century her method remained widely popular.

The introduction of a Scottish Cheddar in the mid-nineteenth century and the establishment of a Dairy School at Kilmarnock in 1889 where cheesemaking could be learnt assured the future of such cheeses. It also, ironically, may have contributed to the current position where highly commercial mass production has almost totally replaced traditional farm-house methods.[2,3]

Today Scotland's dairy industry is by no means small (the liquid milk market in Scotland alone is worth over £200 million a year), but it is considerably smaller than south of the Border. This, in combination with the effects of EEC legislation, has brought Scottish farmers new problems.

The industry has been supported since the 1930s by the Milk Marketing Boards, statutory bodies set up by Act of Parliament to support and promote dairying. The Boards (there are three in Scotland) are obliged to buy all cows' milk produced, and to obtain for the farmer the best possible price.

The advent of the EEC brought great changes in the dairy industry. Farms tended to become larger and more

Opposite: Goat's cheeses made by Mrs Denise Ferguson.
(Della Matheson)

Below: Three little maids . . . make sheep's milk cheese at Humphrey Errington's farm at Ogcastle.
(Della Matheson)

Milking techniques have changed quite considerably . . .
(National Museums of Scotland)

efficient, although there were fewer producers. Guaranteed sales for their milk encouraged farmers to increase their production, with the resultant 'butter mountains' caused by European over-production on a massive scale. In response the EEC commissioners introduced 'dairy quotas' in 1984 – carefully worked out maximum production figures which ensured a gradual reduction in surplus. Quotas are firmly adhered to, with a draconian 'super-levy' payable on milk over quota.

By and large the quota system has worked well, though recently shortage of milk in Scotland has meant the temporary closure of a number of creameries. Dalbeattie Creamery, renowned for its 'choicest' cheeses, has now closed permanently.

Since the 1960s, Scottish Cheddar has been produced in large creameries to a

Cheesemaking, Ayrshire – the old-fashioned way.
(School of Scottish Studies)

minimum standard, usually 18kg (40lb.) blocks. The result, while uniform, offers little by way of choice and none of the old farmhouse favourites. The development has been a progression from the days of World War II, when feeding the nation was paramount, and there was no time for long maturing.

Cheese is graded as 'Choicest' (a grade virtually never awarded now, and in recent years awarded only to the excellent, now defunct Dalbeattie Cheddar), first grade (95 per cent of production, and of a standard which appears to satisfy most major retailers), 1A (which has a weak body or is slightly acid), 1B (slightly curdy), Graded, and 'No Stamp'. This last category will have some spoilage bacteria, sometimes due to a faulty starter culture and sometimes with no apparent cause. It is sent for processing. The man who grades all cheese produced in the Scottish creameries (except that of one farmhouse cheesemaker on Orkney) is George Nicol, who has been working with cheese for 55 years. He now works for the Company of Scottish Cheesemakers, which was incorporated in 1954 in order to improve the quality of Scottish Cheddar.

The cheese is first graded at two months. Certain cheeses – normally the better quality ones – are left to mature while others are selected for more immediate use. 'I use a simple and age-old tool called a cheese iron', explains Mr Nicol. 'One complete turn of the iron, and I can pull out a small core of cheese. First I *smell* it, then I break small pieces off and *feel* it. I rub the cheese between my fingers until it breaks down. If the cheese is too hard, I mark it to be held. The texture can improve with age. Cheese with a weaker body has to be sold at around six months. *Appearance* and *colour* are the final factors in grading cheese, and I look not only at the cheese itself, but at the film on the back of the iron too. The one thing I don't do is *taste* the cheese. After two or three, they all taste the same.'

The vagaries of cheesemaking, even in the highly mechanised and controlled environment of Scotland's modern creameries, demand a constant and

watchful eye. 'Cheesemaking is an art,' says Galloway Creamery Manager, Matthew Glover. 'Most of the success of cheesemaking depends on the starter culture. Pasteurisation destroys the natural lactic acid producing bacteria. These organisms have to be put back in – that is what starter culture is. Here we buy in minute quantities of culture, then develop our own. Other critical factors are the rate of the acid development and the moisture content, and the salting. It is very important to get the salting just right.'

Galloway Creamery, which belongs to Scottish Pride, the marketing arm of the Scottish Milk Marketing Board, is one of Scotland's biggest. The Creamery takes in between 163 000 litres (36 000 gallons) (low season) and 195 000 litres (43 000 gallons) (peak) of milk per day. Most of the milk is made into cheddar cheese through a carefully controlled series of operations. The milk is pasteurised, killing off any possible unwanted bacteria, then starter culture is added back in. The operator now knows exactly what bacteria are present in the milk. Colouring (annatto) is added if the cheese being made is 'red', and the milk stirred in vats to ensure that the annatto is properly distributed. Rennet is mixed in, coagulating the milk within about ¾ hour. The blades in the container are turned to cut the mixture, and at this stage there is the formation of curds and whey. The curds and whey then pass to the cheddaring area, where the

George Nicol, cheese grader for the Company of Scottish Cheesemakers, smelling a core pulled out with the cheese iron.
(Carter Rae)

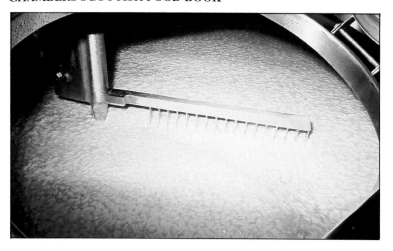

curds fall into deep stainless steel trays while the whey is forced through by sheer pressure of its own weight. The curd becomes increasingly consolidated as it passes through the cutting machine which breaks the curds into chips. Salt (around 5 per cent) is added. Much of this is squeezed out by the end of the cheese-making process, and reduced to around 1·8 per cent. The cheese is then forced into moulds, usually 18kg. (40lb.), and left overnight in presses, where stacked in layers, more whey is forced out. Finally, it is cut, packed and vacuum sealed.

Top: Cutting and scalding the curds, Galloway Creamery.
Above left: The cheddaring texture of the curds.
Above right: The curd is broken into chips.
(Galloway Creamery)

Right: Checking the curd chips.
(Carter Rae)

Opposite top: Wrapping the cheese blocks.
(Carter Rae)

Opposite right: Sheep's milk cheese is enjoying a revival in fashion.
(Della Matheson)

For Galloway Creamery, as for many others, by-products of cheesemaking form an important part of the operation. Here cheese whey is evaporated to whey powder, used in the confectionery industry. This is an important protein source. It can be demineralised to neutralise the acid, giving a very sweet product. This is used in baby foods, chocolate manufacture, biscuits, and also forms the powdery substance which coats the fruit and nuts in some commercial muesli mixtures. At Galloway Creamery there is also a Feta cheese plant. This very low fat, acid cheese is made largely for export, primarily to Iran. This market is unpredictable, and production consequently fluctuates.

Careful planning of production to achieve maximum return is also the concern of small independent cheesemakers, of which Scotland has a fair number, though most concentrate on the production of soft cheeses. The Marwicks of Howgate at Penicuik, Midlothian, began

to make cheese in 1966, as 'Mrs Marwick's hobby'. After twenty years of farm production, the Marwicks' Howgate Creamery has now moved on to an industrial site, which removes the romance but in fact improves consistency.

'We like our products to be as natural as possible,' explained Mrs Marwick. 'Our cream is pasteurised *after* separation.

Inconsistencies have been more or less eliminated since we moved to the industrial unit, which is air conditioned and kept at precise temperatures – like working in a big fridge.

'Our production is dictated by the amount of cream in our orders. Some cream goes into the making of cream cheese, which we also produce rolled in

Humphrey Errington's sheep's milk cheeses are very highly regarded.

(Della Matheson)

oatmeal, pepper or nuts and bran. The skimmed milk goes to making yoghurt, plain or in twelve fruit flavours – and again, we like our product as natural as possible, and we don't add stabilisers. We also make curd cheese – 'Crowdie', which has no fat, and cottage cheese. Sometimes curd cheese has fat added, when we make crowdie and cream or soft cheese.

'Whole milk is also used in our production. With whole milk we make a Camembert-type cheese called Lothian, a Brie-type called Pentland, a peat-smoked soft cheese, and a Gouda-type called Langskaill. We also make goats' milk soft cheese and yoghurt when we can get goats' milk.'

Howgate have made Lothian and Pentland since 1970, but have only recently ironed out their problems of inconsistency. 'There is an enormous demand,' said Mrs Marwick, 'especially from restaurants which feature Scottish menus. This is a big growth area. The cheeses

mature for a week in a maturing room, but we send them out fairly raw.'

Mrs Marwick, like very many of Scotland's cheesemakers, learned her skills at Auchencruive, the West of Scotland Agricultural College. Senior lecturer there for many years was Janet Galloway, now an independent cheese consultant. 'Making a profit out of cheesemaking is no easy task for the small producer,' says Miss Galloway. 'You have to be technically expert, but you also need business acumen and know how to package and market your product too.' This would certainly be endorsed by Mrs Marwick, who has produced a distinctive series of tartan boxes which sell particularly well at shows.

Miss Galloway's technical expertise has been passed on to many of Scotland's producers developing new cheeses – farmers such as Humphrey Errington at Ogcastle, Carnwath. 1986 was the year that saw the launch of Mr Errington's

Cheese is stored under strictly hygienic conditions to mature.
(Della Matheson)

Modern milking methods are employed on the Ogcastle farm.
(Della Matheson)

Lanark Blue on the market – a cheese much resembling Roquefort, and made in time-honoured fashion with sheep's milk.

The vogue for making cheese with sheep and goats' milk is now well established, though Mr Errington's own researches show that sheep's milk cheeses were made around Biggar quite commonly until the end of the eighteenth century. 'The old songs and ballads show that milking the ewes was one of the few activities where young people of both sexes were allowed to be together for lengthy periods of time, away from the Presbyterian eyes of their elders. The results are easy to predict and can probably also be confirmed by parish records.'

The modern hygienic milking parlour at Ogcastle, typical of modern parlours, is a less likely place for romance, while in the creamery itself, high humidity and stainless steel vats are essential to success. Lanark Blue is a mould-ripened (blue) cheese. The penicillium spores come from Italy in liquid form, and are introduced with the rennet at the beginning of the cheesemaking process. The piercing of the cheeses with wires, in the ripening room, allows air to penetrate so that the mould can grow.

More recently Mr Errington has been experimenting with a Gorgonzola-type cheese called Dunsyre. These cheeses, though somewhat variable, are always interesting and at times quite delicious. A third, experimental cheese is Errington's Special, a Scottish version of Gorgonzola Dolce.

The oldest recorded Scottish cheese is 'Caboc', the buttery full-fat oatmeal-coated cheese made by Mrs Stone in Ross-shire. Made originally by Mariota de Ile, daughter of a fifteenth-century Lord of the Isles, the recipe came down through the generations to Mrs Stone, who revived it for her husband and friends and has been supplying the market ever since. Her other products include Hramsa, a cottage cheese with wild garlic leaves in cream (and a low-fat version without the cream); Galic, a soft full-fat cheese with wild garlic leaves, rolled in flaked oats, crumbled almonds and hazelnuts; and Highland Soft Cheese, a full-fat soft cheese.

Joanna Blythman owns a delicatessen in the heart of Edinburgh and has a special passion for cheeses of excellence. She disparages the poor efforts of Scotland in recent years in this regard. 'Until recently, Scottish cheeses were seen by many as a lost cause,' she says. In her view, however, the position is slowly changing. 'Scotland may yet have a long way to go to match the cheesemaking potential of other countries, but there are promising moves in the right direction.'

Among Joanna Blythman's favourites is Bonchester, made at Bonchester Bridge near Hawick, where John Curtis has his own Jersey herd and makes a soft, Coulommiers-type cheese. It is made with unpasteurised milk in a 0·454kg. (1-lb.) round, and has a natural white-mould crust. She also favours Stichill, Sgriob-Ruadh, and Shapinsay. Stichill is made at Kelso by Brenda Leddie from the milk of Jersey cows and, in her words, 'it seems to encapsulate the crumbly rich qualities of authentic Wensleydale with the refreshing tartness of farmhouse Cheshire or Lancashire.' Sgriob-Ruadh (pronounced skib-roo-a) is a tangy farmhouse cheddar from Tobermory, Isle of Mull, while Shapinsay is a 'reliable' farmhouse cheese, somewhere between a cheddar and a Caerphilly in texture. Another ewes' milk cheese is Barac, a semi-hard Dales-type cheese made from unpasteurised ewes' milk. This white Dumfriesshire cheese has a lightly waxed crust and a sweet, nutty flavour.

Goats' milk cheeses have seen a big rise in popularity recently, and with parallel developments in goat farming, look set to make further progress. A promotional

Goat's cheese is enjoying a revival in popularity.

(Della Matheson)

Mary Rollo, a prize-winning butter maker in Fife at the turn of the century.

(Fife Folk Museum, Ceres)

body, the Scottish Goat Product Marketing Co-operative, has been formed to maximise the good reception which goats' milk products have received, while a number of goats' milk cheeses have begun to make their presence felt in the marketplace. Strathrusdale is made at Invergordon, Robrock Roset from Huntly is a wine-dipped mild creamy cheese, and Isle of Sanday is a rich, full-flavoured goats' milk cheese.

The advent of the Single Market in 1992 will bring a new threat to Scotland's dairy markets. 'It is well proven that the British housewife is not really concerned with country of origin, but only with cost,' claims Tim Russell, Marketing Director of the Scottish Milk Marketing Board. 'Milk imported from dairy-rich Ireland will undoubtedly force us to reassess our market position.'

Scottish cheesemakers look set for expansion, though many cheeses still require refinement. But taste in Scotland is changing as the world gets smaller, and a new, exciting market is undoubtedly there for the enterprising cheesemaker.

Ice Cream

It would not be possible to discuss the dairy industry in Scotland without mentioning the remarkable growth of the ice-cream business in the last fifty years. Almost every town and village in the country now has its own locally made *Italian* ice cream – full flavoured, creamy and consumed (considering the climate) in remarkable quantities.

'The Scots are renowned for their sweet tooth,' comments Mr Tino Luca of Musselburgh, one of the most esteemed producers of ice cream in the country.

Mr Luca's father came to Scotland in 1908 from Cassino in Italy. 'Times were bad there, and many Italians in that area left to seek opportunities elsewhere. They went to America – and to Scotland.' Ice-cream making was not an obvious choice of career; even in Italy in those days the confection did not have a high profile. Mr Luca's father learned the art of making ice cream from a Swiss chef at the North British Hotel, Edinburgh and was not slow to see its potential. Looking at the queues outside Luca's on a sunny day, it is clear that he was a man of great foresight.

'The business has revolutionised in the last decade,' comments Mr Luca. 'Nowadays everyone has a freezer, so a lot of our trade is in pre-packed cartons. A few years ago almost all our ice cream was sold in cornets over the counter.

'I think our reputation for quality rests on the fact that we use only the best ingredients – milk fresh from the farm, double cream, butter. We keep everything as natural as possible.

'We get a lot of visitors from the south who make sure they come to buy ice cream from us. They do comment on the extra sweetness, but they come back because they say our standards are so high.'

1. Patrick Rance, *The Great British Cheese Book*, Macmillan, London 1982, p. 91.
2. Annette Hope, *A Caledonian Feast*, Mainstream, Edinburgh 1987, p. 147.
3. Rance, *op. cit.*, p. 91.

Oatmeal Flan with Smoked Salmon and Lanark Blue

Smoked salmon is so good in its natural state that it seems sacrilegious to cook it. It is often served grilled with butter in the far North-West, and very good it is. Using the off-cuts, which can usually be had at a good price, is the sensible way to avoid feelings of guilt. This recipe exploits the interesting affinity between salmon and the excellent blue sheep's milk cheese from Lanark.

Mix the flour and oats, salt lightly, then cut and rub in the butter and lard. Add a little water to make a dough. Refrigerate in a plastic bag until needed.

Roll out the pastry, not too thin, and line the two pastry tins (this pastry is difficult to handle; if it breaks simply patch it together).

Bake blind at Gas 6, 400°F, 205°C, allowing 10 minutes with foil weighted down with beans, and 10 minutes uncovered.

Whip the eggs and egg yolk, then beat in the cream. Dice or slice the salmon and cheese and add to the eggs and cream. Season lightly, being very careful not to add too much salt (Lanark Blue is quite salty).

Fill the pastry tins with the filling and bake at Gas 5, 375°F, 190°C for 30–35 minutes, until the filling is puffed up and set.

Serve hot or cold with a mustard-flavoured mayonnaise and beetroot salad (p. 72).

For the pastry:

(Makes 2 20-cm. (eight-inch) flans)

125g. (5 oz.) flour (plain or wholemeal)
125g. (5 oz.) medium oatmeal
12g. (2½ oz.) butter
12g. (2½ oz.) lard
pinch of salt

For the filling:

2 eggs and 1 egg yolk
150ml. (⅓ pint) double cream
150g. (6 oz.) smoked salmon
100g. (4 oz.) Lanark Blue
salt and white pepper

Dunlop Cheese Puffs

Dunlop cheese is ideal for these savoury choux pastry puffs. Individual breakfast-roll-sized puffs can be filled with stir-fried vegetables and seafood as an interesting first course. Bite-sized puffs filled with crab mayonnaise make marvellous savouries to accompany drinks.

Gently heat the water, salt and butter in a small saucepan until the butter melts.

Sift the flour. Bring the water to the boil, remove from the heat immediately and add all of the flour. Beat with a wooden spoon until the paste is smooth and comes away from the sides of the pan.

Beat over a low heat for up to a minute to dry the dough.

Beat one egg until mixed and reserve. Beat the remaining eggs into the dough one at a time: beat vigorously after each one. Beat in enough of the reserved egg until the dough is shiny and just falls from an inverted spoon.

Mix in the diced cheese and season.

Butter a baking sheet. Use two spoons to make puffs of the desired size. Sprinkle the balls of dough with the grated cheese.

Bake in a very hot oven (Gas 7, 425°F, 220°C) for 25–30 minutes, until they are golden brown.

85g. (3½ oz.) flour
60g. (2½ oz.) butter
150ml. (⅓ pint) water
1 2·5ml spoon (½ teaspoon) salt
3–4 eggs
50g. (2 oz.) Dunlop cheese, diced
2 15ml. spoons (2 tablespoons) Dunlop cheese grated
white pepper, nutmeg

Opposite: Oatmeal Flan with Smoked Salmon and Lanark Blue.

(Victor Albrow)

91

Lanark Blue and Endive Fritters

Deep frying has long been popular in Scotland. This recipe derives mainly from the Chinese spring roll, but it is evidence of how international our food has become that we can readily buy the Middle-Eastern filo pastry. Quantities here are unimportant. Serve as a first course with salad.

filo pastry, frozen or fresh
Belgian endive (chicory)
Lanark Blue
freshly shelled walnuts
walnut or olive oil

Slice the endives into 1·5-cm. (½-inch) rounds and separate the leaves.

Make a salad of these with the cheese, roughly crumbled, and walnuts. Dress with a little walnut or olive oil. No other seasoning is necessary.

Place 3 or 4 15ml. spoons (tablespoons) of the salad on a sheet of pastry. Wrap the parcel so that there are two or three layers all round, and the ends are well tucked in. Refrigerate for an hour or so.

Fry the parcels in plenty of hot oil until they are evenly golden. The cheese should be on the point of melting.

Oatmeal Ice Cream

In the earlier part of this century many thousands of Italians came to Scotland in the search for work. They have greatly enriched our culture, not least with their dairy ice creams. In almost every little town in Scotland there is an Italian café, still making the real thing. This home-made ice cream is very different in texture, but it is worthwhile. An Italian version, with crumbled amaretti (macaroons) and marsala, is equally good.

300ml. (½ pint) each double and single cream
150g. (6 oz.) vanilla sugar
75g. (3 oz.) medium oatmeal, lightly toasted
50g. (2 oz.) granulated sugar
2 15ml. spoons (2 tablespoons) water
2 15ml. spoons (2 tablespoons) malt whisky
(optional, substitute extra water if desired)

Whip the two creams with the vanilla sugar until thick. Freeze as quickly as possible, stirring from time to time.

Make a syrup by boiling the water, or water and whisky, with the granulated sugar for a few minutes. Allow to cool.

When the ice cream is almost frozen, transfer it to a mixing bowl. Beat in the syrup with the oatmeal, making sure it is well mixed.

Freeze until solid. Remove from the refrigerator at least 15–30 minutes before serving.

Frozen Soufflé with Whisky Liqueur

A French confection really, but one which takes the flavour of whisky beautifully.

Wrap a 61-cm (24-inch) strip of greaseproof paper around a soufflé dish so that it protrudes 5–7·5cm (2–3 inches) above the rim. Chill the dish in the freezer.

Sprinkle the sponge fingers with half of the liqueur, on a baking tray.

Beat the egg yolks until they thicken.

Make a syrup with the water and sugar. Boil it vigorously until a few drops put into iced water immediately form coarse threads.

Pour the hot syrup on to the egg yolks in a thin stream, beating constantly. Continue beating until the mixture is thick and smooth, about 10–15 minutes. Fold in the remaining whisky liqueur.

Beat the cream in a chilled bowl until it forms soft peaks.

Gently mix the egg-yolk mixture and whipped cream until no trace of white is visible.

Line the base and sides of the soufflé dish with the sponge fingers, trimming them as necessary.

Spoon in the soufflé mixture to the rim of the dish. Chill in the freezer for 20 minutes. Meanwhile refrigerate the remaining mixture, then fill the collar, smoothing the surface with a spatula.

Freeze overnight, or for at least 6 hours. Transfer to the refrigerator 15 minutes before serving to allow it to soften.

Immediately before serving sprinkle the top with toasted oatmeal and remove the paper collar.

For 6–8:

18 sponge fingers
6 egg yolks
225g. (¹/₂lb.) sugar
6 15ml. spoons (6 tablespoons) Drambuie or Glayva
35ml. (¹/₃ cup) water
300ml. (¹/₂ pint) double cream
1 15ml. spoon (1 tablespoon) cocoa powder (unsweetened)
1 15ml. spoon (1 tablespoon) toasted oatmeal

6. Grain-Cherishing Tradition

It was pleasant to me to find, that 'oats', the 'food of the horses', were so much used as the food of the people in Dr Johnson's own town.[1]

Oatmeal is much cherished in Scotland, despite the disappearance of porridge from many of today's breakfast tables. It is a grain that evokes historical memory and sentiment. The vigour and endurance of fourteenth-century Scottish armies – each man marching with a small sack of oatmeal and a metal plate on which to cook it – were attributed to this staple. In Shetland a large oatcake called the 'dreaming cake' was traditionally thrown over the bride's head, with guests scrambling for the pieces. Many a university student also had reason to be thankful for oatmeal: it was the chief provision (along with a barrel of salted herring) they carried to Edinburgh, Glasgow, Aberdeen and St Andrews at the beginning of each term.

Until World War II, oats were one of the three principal cereal crops grown in Scotland and throughout the UK. The agricultural change from oats to barley, which began at the end of the War, quickly gained momentum, ultimately changing the balance: today in Scotland the land given over to oats and mixed grains is just over 29 000 hectares (71 660 acres), while spring and winter barley account for almost 400 000 hectares (98 840 acres).

Oats have a high protein content, as well as possessing more oil and crude fibre than barley, wheat or rye; and oats have always been considered a good way

Opposite: Blair Atholl. A well-restored working mill.
(Carter Rae)

Below: Harvesting grain on the Black Isle.
(Highlands and Islands Development Board)

A tea break during the harvest at Blelock Farm, Perthshire, 1934.

(Harry Davidson)

of 'heating the blood'. The use of oats in cooking was, and still can be, quite imaginative. Skirlie, made with medium-ground oatmeal, onions, seasoning and either suet or roast dripping, was served as a main course or with meat or game or used as a poultry stuffing; oatmeal soup, still made today in Orkney, combines a small amount of the grain with carrot, leek and turnip in stock; while Athol Brose, a drink consumed in quantity at Hogmanay, was based on an oatmeal paste which was sieved and mixed with honey, whisky and water. All of these recipes survive today in traditional cookery books. The habit persists of using oatmeal to eke out the rations (a particularly useful trick with stewed mince) and as a coating for herring. The grain is also used in puddings. This practice undoubtedly had its origins not in the humble dwelling but in the 'big house.' Cranachan is a good example (see recipe p. 76).

Oatcakes were once the nearest thing to bread made by the Scots, though the Orcadians made a flat loaf or bannock, from 'bere' or barley meal. A number of recipes have also survived for oatmeal pancakes, biscuits and cakes. The oatcake, eaten with a selection of Scottish cheeses, as an accompaniment to broth, or even with jams or honey, still requires a deft touch in the making. Tradition demands its baking not in an oven but on a girdle, a flat circular iron disc, which in days past hung over an open fire. The word probably comes from the old French *grédil* meaning grid iron although the hot stones used for cooking bread by the early Gaels were called *greadeal*. Once baked, oatcakes were often toasted on a rack in front of the peat fire, before being eaten. The basic ingredients of the oatcake – oatmeal, lard, salt, soda and water – remain unchanged but the size and shape can vary, from thin triangles to thick rounds. Oatmeal is ground in a number of different 'cuts' (sizes), from superfine to pinhead. The former is particularly suited to gruel, the age-old invalid food, while the latter can be used in forms of skirlie or even poultry stuffing. Small mills, like the Montgarrie Mills at Alford, Aberdeenshire, grind enough oatmeal from farms in Kincardine, Aberdeen, Banff and Moray to satisfy local needs and tastes – they offer six different cuts of the grain. The water-wheel is still operational at Montgarrie, though it is supplemented with an auxiliary paraffin engine, and visitors are welcome to watch the milling process, by arrangement.

The move towards healthier eating and restoration of water-driven mills in various parts of the country, have helped to reintroduce oats into the Scottish diet. One of the people responsible for this surge of interest in old mills is John Ridley, a hydraulic engineer, who in 1976 started renovating the old mill at Blair Atholl, near Pitlochry. His belief in simple and wholesome food, coupled with his enchantment with the old milling mechanism, was infectious and he now acts as a consultant to other similar restorations in Scotland.

The Mill at Blair Atholl dates back to 1613, a time when landowners were required to provide a mill for their tenants and workers. Country mills of this type were put out of business not only by improved transport, which meant that grain could be taken to towns and larger mills, but by a World War I Act requiring white flour to be standard. The inability of the small water-mill to accede to the Act put them out of business. Blair Atholl ceased milling in 1929, and the building

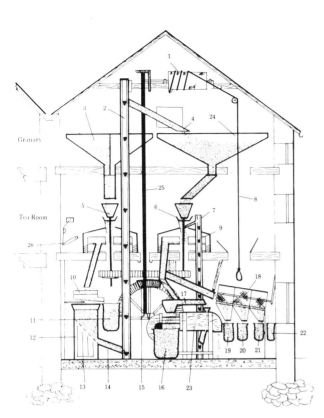

1   Drum for sack hoist.
2   Main Bucket Elevator.
3   Hopper for Oats.
4   Grain from Oatmeal Machine in basement, delivered by elevator to hopper feeding grinding stones.
5   Small hopper on stone vat, supplied from main hopper above.
6   'Shoe'.
7   Small bucket elevator returning lumps for re-grinding.
8   Sack hoist.
9   'Runner' stone.
10   Sieve (Rattler, shaker) separating dust from grain.
11   Dust bag.
12   Oatmeal machine separating chaff from grain.
13   Chaff box.
14   Grain (now called groats) feed to buckets of main elevator.
15   Pit-wheel and wallower.
16   Sack collecting oatmeal or flour.
17   Sieve (Rattler, shaker) separating lumps from ground flour or oatmeal.
18   'Reel' or 'Wire Machine' dressing or grading flour.
19   Fine flour sack.
20   Medium flour sack.
21   Course flour sack.
22   Sack collecting lumps.
23   'Sids' machine, diverting lumps into small elevator for regrinding.
24   Hopper for wheat or groats (oat grains).
25   Main vertical driving shaft.
26   Mill water gate control. For starting and stopping the mill.

Diagram of the restored Blair Atholl Mill.

(John Ridley)

subsequently became storage for cattle food and coal.

Blair Atholl's restored mill now provides a steady flow of oatmeal and wholemeal flour products, and its oatmeal has even been shipped to wholefood shops in the US. The philosophy of simple and wholesome food is carried through to its own bakery and tearoom, presided over by Josephine Ridley, the miller's wife. Flour milled on the premises is used for such traditional favourites as cloutie dumpling, scones, shortbread, flapjacks, biscuits and cakes. The mill is open from 1 April to 31 October and visitors to the premises are welcome to watch the restored mill in operation.

Although wholemeal flour is more widely accepted for baking – and in some cases has made the fortunes of many small bakers catering for wholefood customers – white flour is still very much preferred for traditional Scottish baking. Shortbread, like oatcakes a popular tourist purchase, is not quite the same made with wholemeal flour, and the range of mince and steak pies beloved for generations, would seem unnatural with brown pastry. Although wheat is grown in Scotland (the amount of land has been steadily increasing because of EEC levies on imports) and about 102 000 hectares (252 047 acres) are now under cultivation the climate makes the quality of the grain uncertain. The high consistency of North American grain is still preferred by many in spite of the EEC levies.

Robert Burns, the national bard, once referred to Scotland as the 'Land o' Cakes'. He was, in fact, talking about oatcakes not the diverse range of sweet biscuits and cakes which have become synonymous with the Scottish high tea. Although the campaign to reduce sugar in the diet has undoubtedly affected the daily intake of many of the more luxurious cakes, the habit still persists of indulging the sweet tooth on Sunday. Kenneth Klessa, who runs a small independent bakery in Edinburgh's Clerk Street, says

'Scots treat themselves at the weekend – the rest of the week they eat rolls and pies.' His bakery, Francis Irvine, has been in the family since the beginning of the century and on a Saturday morning there are lengthy queues at his door stocking up on his specialities: vanilla slices, custard pies, mince pies and rolls. All of his baking is traditional – the recipe for the apple charlotte on display in the shop hasn't changed since the days of his great-grandfather – the Hollywood tart (iced currants and walnuts on pastry), came in with his grandfather. Individual meat pies, a favourite Scottish main course, also still retain their popularity. The bakers working in the Francis Irvine shop make 30 dozen pies every day from

Weighing out the freshly ground meal at Blair Atholl.
(Carter Rae)

Monday to Saturday although, as Mr Klessa reports, the content of these has changed slightly over the years. In his grandfather's day, rusks were used to swell the meat content; nowadays, the pies have a soya base.

Increased concern with nutrition has altered the demand for certain grains. 'Over the last ten years there has been a swing towards health foods,' said Fiona Horsburgh, owner of Roots, an Edinburgh shop. The variety of grains and cereals sold in her shop and other similar establishments is not typically Scottish – only ten per cent of the grain sold in Roots is home-grown. The new-found palate for grains like Bulgar wheat, which comes from the Middle East, can be attributed, in Edinburgh at least, to university and college students who created the demand. Their influence can still be noted during term-time by bakers like Kenneth Klessa, whose output of baked loaves is equally divided between white and wholemeal.

'When the students go away,' he says, 'the brown sales slump.'

The use of wholemeal flour in baking has spread from the small health food shops and bakeries to the larger manufacturers, who now attempt to offer something more imaginative than the sliced white loaf. The trend for supermarkets to follow the expansion into whole foods will also continue in the opinion of Fiona Horsburgh, who predicts that 'supermarkets in the future will veer away from additive-type foods and concentrate on healthy foods.' But if the trend towards healthier eating is changing the traditional diet and bakery shop, so, too, is the increasing influence from the Continent. Italian and French bakers flourish in Edinburgh, while in Glasgow a French patisserie does a lively trade in Byres Road, one of the main areas of student population.

Glasgow, it is reliably reported, has always had more of a sweet tooth than the

The delights of the traditional tearoom, Largs.

(Scottish Tourist Board)

Capital. It is a known fact that Glasgow bakers add more sugar to their products than do their Edinburgh counterparts. The love of sweet cakes is one reason why one of the city's newest bakeries, The California Cake and Cookie Company, has prospered. The most popular items in their range – American 'Brownies' and 'Banana Cake' – have a high sugar content. Glasgow, however, is not alone in taking to these favourite recipes from abroad – California Cake and Cookie sell through one of the national supermarket chains.

There is good reason for Glasgow's love of cakes and tea. At the turn of the century, the city was better endowed with

Home baking at Duart Castle Tearooms, Mull.
(Scottish Tourist Board)

quality tearooms than London, as one writer reported:

> What wonder if the gangrel Scot from the Clyde returns with pleasure to his town, where he may lunch on lighter fare than steak and porter for the sum of fivepence [2·5p] amid surroundings that remind him of a pleasant home.
>
> Glasgow, in truth, is a very Tokio for tearooms. Nowhere can one have so much for so little, and nowhere are such places more popular or frequented.[2]

The tearooms of Glasgow were remarkable not only because they offered an inexpensive and socially acceptable alternative to the city's pubs, but because of their interior decoration. Miss Cranston's Willow Tea Rooms in Sauchiehall Street, designed by Charles Rennie Mackintosh, was the most famous. Each table featured a three-tier cake stand filled with scones, pancakes and small cakes – the accompaniment to a main meal of cold meat or possibly a kipper or fish and chips. Other tearooms were less ambitious in decor but equally acceptable:

> . . . The arrangement of the tables is pleasant. These are not the bleak marble things of the Edinburgh Café or an A.B.C. shop, but are made of wood, and are spread with fair white cloths, and set with flowers and china. The scones and cakes, too, are there at hand, to have and to hold.[3]

While Glasgow enjoyed the delights of Miss Cranston's tearoom, Edinburgh in the early 1900s was enjoying the novelty of a similar facility at Jenners. The well-known Princes Street store, which had burned down just before Christmas in 1892, had been rebuilt with a mezzanine tearoom decorated in cream and gold. A Ladies' Cloakroom, and a writing and 'retiring room', were adjacent. In addition to taking tea accompanied by freshly baked scones and cakes from the store's own bakehouse, women could rest from the stresses of shopping, write letters and even receive parcels delivered from other shops in the city.

The Jenners bakery produced classic shortbread, mince pies and even plum puddings, all of which found their way into the annual Christmas catalogue. In 1938, the Christmas catalogue was advertising a dozen boxed mince pies for three shillings (15p) (plus ninepence (5p) postage) and five-pound (2·27kg.) plum puddings ('from a forty-year-old recipe') for seven shillings and sixpence (37·5p). The plum puddings and mince pies are no more, but Jenners still have their own bakery which produces fresh bread daily in addition to Madeira and ginger cakes, fruit slices and wedding cakes. The tearooms of the cities, of course, offered a contrast to home catering and the baking skills of the average Scottish cook. Proficiency in baking was once an important requisite for Scottish brides: no young woman began marriage without her baking boards, rolling pin, mixing bowl and girdle. The reputation has lingered through the years, a 'light touch' with the baking being considered the supreme accolade.

The range of cakes and biscuits, breads and pastry, for which Scotland has won a reputation, are to some extent still tied to the region of origin. The Selkirk Bannock, a yeast bread made with sultanas and raisins, said to have been a favourite of Queen Victoria's, is more readily available in the town that gives it its name than elsewhere (see recipe p. 106), while the Forfar Bridie, with its filling of rump steak and onions, harks back to the days when the town was the centre of the Aberdeen Angus cattle trade. Dundee Cake, a fruit cake decorated with blanched almonds, has been a popular tea-time cake since the late nineteenth century, and along with shortbread enjoys a place as a popular tourist gift. Butteries, a rich bread roll from Aberdeenshire (see recipe p. 105), have become more universal, alongside the French croissant: in comparison the 'Carvie' biscuit, made with caraway seeds and eaten with cheese, is an old Orkney speciality that is not generally available. Visitors to Orkney will find it at Muir's of Orkney, Stromness, who keep the islands' tradition going with a range of biscuits

made with wholemeal flour and oatmeal. Scotland is, indeed, still a 'Land o' Cakes'.

Top: Border Tart – an old favourite.

(Victor Albrow)

Above: A travelling baker, Ayrshire.

(Cunningham District Council Museum Service, North Ayrshire Museum, Saltcoats)

1. James Boswell, *Life of Dr Johnson*, 1791, Everyman ed., Vol. 1, p. 628.
2. James Hamilton Muir, *Glasgow in 1901*, William Hodge & Co., Glasgow 1901, p. 166.
3. *Ibid.*, p. 168.

Introduction to Baking

In spite of the move towards 'healthier' eating, with its inherent prejudice against white flour, fats and sugar, the traditions of Scottish baking, as we have seen, show no signs of impending extinction. It seems, rather, that the way of using cakes and breads has changed. High tea, or even the more English afternoon tea with cakes and scones, are indeed now rare treats. Instead we are beginning to recognise that some of our traditional recipes are splendid for breakfasts, and others make perfect desserts to crown a good meal. Seen in this way, an intriguing analogy can be drawn with many French recipes, suggesting a cross-fertilisation of ideas which is easy to divine. So it seems quite appropriate to start with basic pastry recipes using the French methods which set off our natural produce to such good effect.

Puff Pastry

Commercial puff pastry is fine for rustic pies, but this fine butter pastry is from a different world. It is much easier to achieve than most people realise, and is one of the most satisfying things to make.

For 450g. (1lb.) pastry:

225g. (¹/₂lb.) plain flour
25g. (1 oz.) butter at room temperature
225g. (¹/₂lb.) chilled butter
150ml. (¹/₄ pint) (scant cup) water
1 5ml. spoon (1 teaspoon) salt
flour for rolling

Make the basic pastry. Put the flour in a large bowl with the salt, make a crater in the centre and add the butter at room temperature, cut up in pieces, and the water.

Mix the ingredients with the tips of your fingers, very gradually incorporating the flour until a ball of dough is formed.

Knead the ball of dough (which should be quite soft) on a floured board, gently and very briefly.

Make two deep incisions in the dough with a sharp knife, and refrigerate it in a plastic bag for an hour or two.

Remove the dough and chilled butter from the refrigerator. Immediately slide the butter into a large plastic bag, and beat it with a rolling pin until you have a 15-cm. (6-inch) square.

Flour the board and roll the pastry to form a square about 25cm. (9 inches) in diameter.

Place the square of butter in the centre of the pastry, so that you have a diamond within a square.

Fold the corners of the pastry over the butter to form an envelope. Press the edges together gently. The butter must be completely enclosed, but it does not matter if the pastry overlaps.

Flour the board, and carefully roll the pastry and butter until you have a rectangle of 45cm. (18 inches) by 25cm (9 inches) extending away from you.

Fold the pastry in three like a letter, bringing the top edge down towards you, then folding the bottom edge over. Now turn this rectangle through a quarter revolution in a clockwise direction.

Roll the pastry again to a rectangle of 45cm. (18 inches) by 25cm. (9 inches). Fold and turn it exactly as above.

The pastry has now been given the first two of its six 'turns'. Refrigerate in its plastic bag for up to an hour.

Roll, fold and turn the pastry again as above, again giving it two turns.

Refrigerate the pastry in its plastic bag again for at least 30 minutes, or several hours if necessary.

At least 30 minutes before it is to be used, take the pastry from the refrigerator and give it two further turns.

Prepare the pastry for baking by rolling it carefully to a thickness of a little less than 6mm (¼ inch).

Cut the pastry *very cleanly* to the desired size and shape with a sharp knife or cutter (it is most important to cut a clean edge or the pastry will not rise).

Brush the surface with beaten egg, being careful not to allow the egg to flow over the edge.

Bake in a hot oven (Gas 7, 425°F, 220°C) for 25 minutes. If the top browns too rapidly, cover with foil for the last 10 minutes.

NOTE: The object is to produce even layers of pastry and butter. A gentle touch with the roller is needed to avoid smashing through the layers. Use plenty of flour during rolling.

Shortcrust Pastry

This basic shortcrust pastry is endlessly versatile. It has only a touch of sweetness, and so can be used for all manner of tarts and pies.

For 450g. (1lb.) pastry:

225g. (¹/₂lb.) plain flour
175g. (6 oz.) butter
1 egg
2 5ml. spoons (2 teaspoons) sugar
1 5ml. spoon (1 teaspoon) salt
1 15ml. spoon (1 tablespoon) cold water

Sift the flour into a large baking bowl. Add the salt and sugar.

Make a crater in the centre of the flour. Add the egg, and the butter at room temperature cut into 6 or 8 pieces.

Mix the ingredients with the tips of the fingers, working quickly. Add the water and continue mixing until a ball of pastry is formed.

Remove the pastry to a well-floured board and finish mixing by kneading it briefly with the ball of the right hand, flicking it over and back with the left hand.

Refrigerate the pastry in a plastic bag for at least a few hours before rolling out and cooking according to the instructions given in individual recipes.

Sweet Shortcrust Pastry

This is the shortcrust pastry *de luxe*, for rich fruit tarts such as the blaeberry tart on p. 77. It is quite sweet, and must be watched carefully when baking, as it burns easily.

For 450g. (1lb.) pastry:

generous 225g. (¹/₂lb.) plain flour
50g. (2 oz.) powdered almonds
100g. (4 oz.) butter
1 egg
50g. (2 oz.) vanilla sugar
pinch of salt

Proceed exactly as outlined in the preceding recipe, using a little water to bring the dough together if necessary.

These shortcrust pastries can be kept in the refrigerator for up to a week, or frozen for about a month, if tightly sealed in a plastic bag. Allow plenty of time for the pastry to relax at room temperature before rolling out.

Butteries

This recipe is virtually identical to that for the French croissant. Though it takes a little time it is easy and well worthwhile. The finished rolls can be frozen either before the final proving or after, for a few days.

Mix the yeast with the sugar and a little water, and allow it to work for 10–20 minutes.

Sift the flour into a warm bowl. Add the yeast and sugar, the salt, and the rest of the water gradually, working well with the tips of your fingers until it is well mixed.

Cover the bowl with a damp cloth, and put it in a warm place until it rises to twice its size. This usually takes 2–3 hours.

Deflate the dough and chill it.

Divide the butter into 3 portions. Beat each in turn with a rolling pin so that the butter is soft but still chilled.

Roll the dough to a rectangle approximately 23cm. (9 inches) by 45cm. (18 inches).

Spread the first portion of butter over the dough in pieces, as evenly as possible.

Fold in three and roll out as for puff pastry, turning the dough through 90 degrees first.

Repeat this process twice more, using the 2 remaining portions. Chill the dough for 30 minutes between each turn and fold.

Finally roll the dough to a thickness of about 6mm (¼ inch). Divide into whatever shapes and sizes you prefer. Place these on a buttered baking tray and put it a warm place for the final rise (about 30 minutes).

When they have risen, brush the surface with milk or beaten egg. Bake in a hot oven (Gas 7, 425°F, 220°C) for 25 minutes, or until they are well puffed up and evenly golden in colour.

450g. (1lb.) plain flour
1 packet fast-acting yeast
1 15ml. spoon (1 tablespoon) caster sugar
1 5ml. spoon (1 teaspoon) (scant) salt
450ml. (³/₄ pint) tepid water
350g. (12 oz.) butter (best quality) or 175g.
(6 oz.) butter and 175g. (6 oz.) lard

Crullas

These doughnuts, traditionally associated with Aberdeen, resemble the Spanish choros, delicious at breakfast with strong, fresh coffee.

Beat the butter to a cream. Beat the eggs and add these with the sugar to the butter. Mix well.

Stir in the flour until the mixture is thick enough to roll out.

Cut the dough into strips 10–12 cm. (4–5 inches) long. Make two lengthwise cuts in the centre of each, and fold the outer strips around the central strip, wet the edges and seal (it should look plaited).

Fry in hot vegetable oil until golden brown. Sprinkle with vanilla sugar and serve hot.

100g. (4 oz.) butter
100g. (4 oz.) caster sugar
4 eggs
100g. (4 oz.) (approx.) flour

Border Tart

The traditional version of this sweet tart is based on a flaky yeast dough like that used in Aberdeen butteries, but a shortcrust pastry shell works just as well. The filling consists of an egg custard poured on top of marzipan and dried fruits. This sort of tart is common in the north of France. Often almonds are added, as in *mirlitons* or the wonderful Norman pear and apple tarts.

450g. (1lb.) shortcrust pastry (page 104)

For the filling:

2 eggs
1 egg yolk
25g. (1 oz.) vanilla sugar
300ml. (1/2 pint) milk
100g. (4 oz.) marzipan
50g. (2 oz.) mixed peel, chopped
25g. (1 oz.) flaked almonds
50g. (2 oz.) sultanas

Beat the eggs with the sugar.

Bring the milk to just below simmering point. Pour it on to the egg mixture, beating constantly. Allow to cool.

Roll out the pastry and line an 8-inch tart tin. Roll out the scraps to make a lattice design or other cut-out shapes according to whim.

Roll out the marzipan and with it line the base of the tart. Add the chopped peel and almonds, and pour on the custard.

Place the pastry shapes or lattice work on top. Bake in a hot oven (Gas 6, 400°F, 200°C) for 10 minutes. Reduce the heat to Gas 5, 375°F, 190°C for a further 20 minutes. The pastry shapes or lattice may be iced before serving.

Selkirk Bannock

This festive fruitbread is a genuine and worthy survivor. It used to be made by enriching bread dough from the local baker with butter and dried fruits, a method analagous to the French brioche. Selkirk Bannock is ostensibly less rich than brioche, containing less butter and no eggs, but it is in practice a fine and satisfying teabread.

900g. (2lb.) flour
100g. (4 oz.) lard
100g. (4 oz.) butter
225g. (8 oz.) granulated sugar
450ml. (3/4 pint) milk
450g. (1lb.) mixed sultanas and seedless
  raisins
50g. (2 oz.) candied orange peel, chopped
2 packets instant yeast
pinch salt
beaten egg for glazing

Sift the flour into a large baking bowl. Add the salt and yeast.

Melt the butter and lard in the milk. Allow this mixture to cool to blood heat (99°F, 37°C).

Pour the milk and fat into a well in the centre of the flour. Mix the dough.

Knead the dough on a floured board for 5 minutes. Return it to the bowl, cover with a cloth and set it to rise in a warm place until it doubles in volume.

Knead the risen dough on the floured board, working in the fruit, peel and sugar.

Shape into two flattish rounds. Put these on a buttered baking tray. Allow them to rise in a warm place until well risen (about 30 minutes).

Bake in a hot oven (Gas 7, 425°F, 220°C) for 15 minutes. Reduce the heat to Gas 5, 375°F, 190°C, and bake until golden brown, and the centre is dry when pierced with a skewer (about 1 hour). Near the end of this period brush with beaten egg.

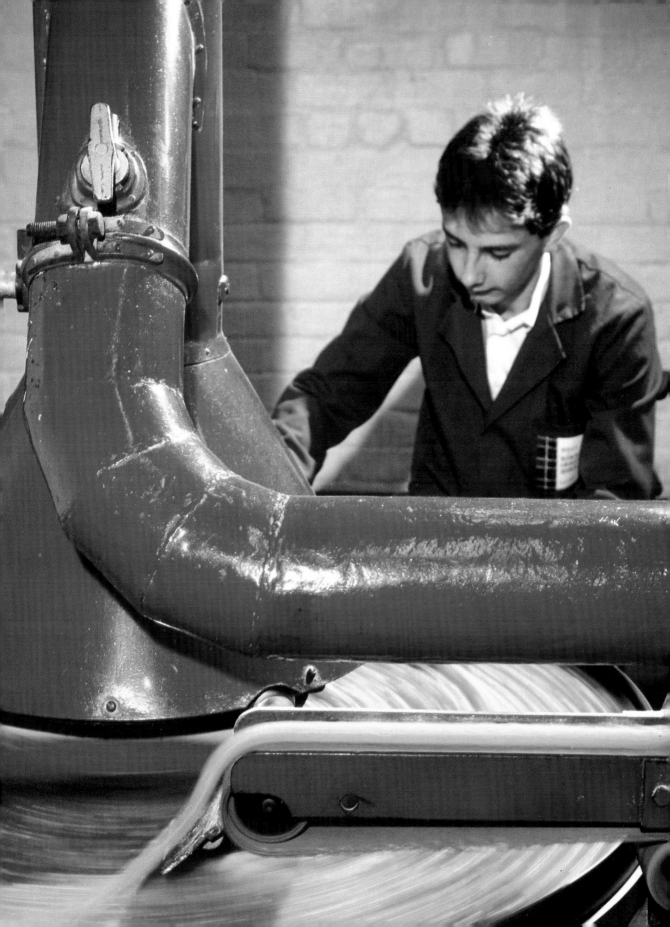

7. Sweeties - A National Indulgence

Here's ginge-bread, confections and
  tablets.
Wha'll buy my dainty plock pies?[1]

Berwick Cockles and Edinburgh Rock, Moffat Toffee and Hawick Balls, Jeddart Snails and Soor Plooms – the names of Scotland's traditional 'sweeties' are as colourful as the confections themselves. Ever since the fifteenth century, when sugar began to be imported in quantity, the Scots have indulged their passion for hard boilings, sticky toffee and creamy tablet. It is a habit which persists despite discouragement from dentists worried about tooth decay.

The very first manufacturing confectioner to set up trade in Edinburgh was an unnamed Italian who in 1665 was given a licence to make 'confeits'. But before that, the Town Council was issuing free sweets on special occasions: to celebrate the coming of age of King James VI, on 14 May 1587, the Provost and Bailies of Edinburgh set up a table in the High Street to dispense free bread, wine and sweets to the town folk. Two years later, when the King brought home his bride, Anne of Denmark, the Council invested £3. 2s 8d [£3.125] on twelve boxes of sweets to scatter about as the royal couple entered the city.

Tablet was sold in the streets of the capital in the eighteenth century, and in Glasgow, too, where sugar-refining was an important industry: the Sweetie Wives, who made their own confections, were a familiar sight in both the streets and the markets. The Border towns also had women who liked making sweets and some of the most familiar confections originated in that locality in the nineteenth century. 'The locals have thrived on Hawick Balls and Berwick Cockles for years,' said Jim McCrone, manager of Hills of Hawick Ltd.

Smith's is a confectionery manufacturer whose business was built on Hawick Balls, the dark brown peppermint-flavoured boilings, once called Taffy Rock Bools. Original recipes for the bools have been lost but it is known that two women, Jessie McVittie and Aggie Lamb, introduced the sweet for the first time in their shops in Hawick. Little did they imagine that the bools would become so famous: not only do Hawick Balls allegedly inspire prowess at rugby, a tin of the sweets has also been buried at the South Pole during an Antarctic expedition.

Jessie made the Rock Bools in her shop at Drumlanrig Square, Hawick in the 1850s as well as Black Sticky Taffy and White Peppermint Taffy. It is said she stretched her Rock Bool mixture and hung it on a nail stuck in the wall, where she could keep an eye on it from her shop counter. As the mixture slowly slid to the ground, Jessie carried on with her housework and tended to customers, until such time as the mixture fell close to the floor when she would suddenly get hold of it, give it a twist and a stretch and hang it over the nail again. This method of 'pulling' was repeated over and over.

Soor Plooms, believed to have originated in Galashiels, are another popular boiling because in Mr McCrone's words, they 'get the juices going in people's mouths.' Tart and lime-coloured, these sweets contain a lot of tartaric acid to give them a tangy flavour. They are particularly popular with the elderly. Berwick Cockles, red-striped peppermint sweets shaped like cockles 'that melt in your mouth', are held in equal esteem, their fame stretching both north and south of the Border.

Small confectioners like Smith's continue a tradition that relies both on the tourist 'gift' industry and the well-known Scottish sweet tooth. And the character of these traditional sweets relies heavily on early methods of manufacture. 'Our sweets have a better and more traditional taste because the sugar gets slightly burnt when we are cooking them,' Says Mr

Previous page: Mixing 'soor plooms' at Hills of Hawick Ltd.

(Ronn Ballantyne)

McCrone. Modern factories clean boil the sugar.' Smith's got the recipes for Berwick Cockles, Soor Plooms and Black Bullets from Ferguson's, an Edinburgh firm which closed down in 1985. Ferguson's chief sweet boiler now works in the Hills of Hawick factory.

Alexander Ferguson ('Sweetie Sandy'), was one of many successful nineteenth-century Scottish confectioners. He had learned to make sweets at his mother's knee while growing up in Doune and it was on the flip of a coin that he chose to set up his first business in Edinburgh in the West Bow. If not for that legendary toss, Edinburgh Rock, which Sandy is credited with discovering, would have been called 'Glasgow Rock'. It is said that this particular confection, which now travels to all corners of the globe, was discovered quite by accident: Sweetie Sandy had unintentionally left a piece of confection lying about for some months. The oversight had resulted in the confection turning soft. It is the softness which today still distinguishes Edinburgh Rock (along with the soft pastel colours) from the hard lettered sticks which appear on so many sea-fronts.

A number of confectioners now manufacture Edinburgh Rock, one of the largest being Ross's of Edinburgh, a firm started by James Ross in 1880 in a small shop near Edinburgh University. In the early years, James Ross concentrated on making tablet and similar products. It was not until 1947, when sugar rationing was relaxed, that the firm was able to undertake its long-held ambition of making Edinburgh Rock. Their first production of the sweet coincided with the first Edinburgh Festival and, within three weeks, all the rock they had made was sold out.

Hand dipping chocolates in Duncan's factory in 1918.

(Duncans of Edinburgh)

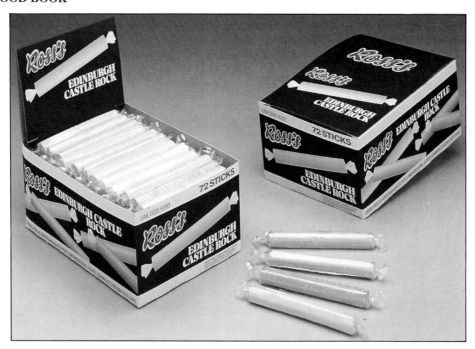

A popular sweet invented by accident.

(Ross's of Edinburgh)

When Graham Ross, great-grandson of the firm's founder, made a recent calculation of the firm's present output of rock, it stood at five million sticks yearly! 'We as a company have deliberately set out to attract the tourist market. We still sell Edinburgh Rock out of a jar, but we put it into tartan boxes for the first Festival and since then everyone else has been putting it in tartan boxes, too.' Ross's 'Edinburgh Castle Rock' is exported to a number of Commonwealth countries and is also sold in France and Holland.

Although recipes for Edinburgh Rock are readily available – it is really nothing more than sugar, water, colouring, flavouring and cream of tartar – expertise is required in the making. There is more than a bit of truth to the old saying that 'it takes ten years to make a good sugar boiler.' As for the pulling, that, too, requires competence. Once the sugar, cream of tartar and colouring have been mixed and boiled, the mixture is poured on to a large rectangular table where it cools off slowly, turning from transparent to opaque. Flavouring is added during the cooling and mixing stage, and once the mass has become tacky it is fixed to a machine for pulling. Final stages of pulling are done by hand either on a stone slab or from a hook fixed to the wall.

Chocolate did not begin to feature in Scottish sweet making until the middle of the nineteenth century when slab chocolate for eating became popular. Prior to that date, chocolate was known only as a drink. By the end of the century, however, chocolate was being manufactured on a larger scale: one small factory which eventually grew into a large business at this time, was Duncans in Edinburgh's Beaverhall Road. This confectionery business was started in Dundee in 1861 by Mary Duncan and her eldest son, William. It grew and in 1927 became part of the Rowntree Company of York. Duncans' repertoire of sweets in the 1930s included a variety of buttered goods like 'Buttered Almonds' and Walnuts, Pralines and Bon-Bons, boilings, rocks and toffees and sweets which they classed as 'Crisps' (lemon, blackcurrant, honey and butter and mint) and 'Satin Goods' (Raspberry Ices, Orange and Lemon Slices, Fig Balls and Chocolate Pralines). All of these sweets were sold by weight from glass jars, a pound (454g.) of Chocolate Pralines costing 10½d (less than 5p). Their chocolates could also be bought by weight, though many were packaged in boxes.

In the 1960s, at the height of their success, Duncans employed 2000 people in their Edinburgh factory in the production of bulk chocolate, Rowntree's Dairy Box chocolates, and Walnut Whips. They also packaged Easter Eggs in quantity. Rationalisation of the Rowntree business in 1987 saw the closure of the Edinburgh factory. It was, however, re-opened in 1988 as a separate company, Duncans of Edinburgh. The range of chocolate products to come from the re-established firm, reflects the market swing away from some of the mass-produced chocolate bars to a product more likely to attract the discerning. Specialist chocolate shops, dealing in both imported and English hand-dipped, moulded and enrobed chocolates (many of which are sold by weight as in days of old) are taking their place alongside gourmet food shops. Duncans' new product line reflects their bid for this market. Although they are once again making three of their best sellers – Parisian Creams (fondant creams coated with plain chocolate), and Hazelnut and Orange Cream Bars – the company has also launched new sweets like Orange Curaçao Bon Bons, Apricot Brandy Truffles and Chocolate Ginger Pralines.

One Scottish sweet, more traditionally cooked at home, is tablet made with milk (see recipe p. 112.) This long-established favourite is also made commercially, and more recently Scottish Goat Products Ltd, Newtonmore have been marketing a tablet made with goats' milk. Islay Tablet is described as 'low fat', its main ingredient being goats' milk produced from a herd of Anglo-Nubian goats. The flavourings of this particular tablet are many and include such well-known products as Islay malt whisky and Drambuie.

Border Country Cousins in Coldstream, who also make tablet commercially, and from traditional recipes, flavour their product with a variety of whiskies. 'We have to be careful how we put the whisky into the mixture,' said the firm's owner, John C. Balfour. 'It took us six months of experimenting before we got it right. If the mixture is too hot then the whisky evaporates.'

Scotch tablet is more traditional than fudge, though fudge has found its niche. It is also sold in a variety of flavourings, including rum and raisin and walnut. Border Country Cousins make fudge and tablet for sale in National Trust properties in Scotland and gift shops, venues quite alien to the market-stalls and small shops which formerly prospered. Other mouth-watering sweets like butterscotch, treacle toffee, striped balls, gobstoppers and countless other old and familiar varieties can still be purchased by weight from a display of wide-necked jars in many small shops around the country, and in one place at least you can still see some of these sweets being made. Dee Valley Confectioners in Station Square, Ballater have a special viewing window for visitors to their factory. Modern machinery makes sweet production more efficient than in years past but the sweeties taste the same.

1. An old street cry, 'Edinburgh Folk Have Long Been Great Sweetie Hands' by David Fergus in the *Edinburgh Evening News*, 28 April 1962.

An abundance of old-fashioned boilings.
(Ronn Ballantyne)

Butterscotch

For those who wish to try their hand at home sweet-making (a splendid diversion for children on a dreich day) here is a recipe for one of the best and most typical.

450g. (1lb.) brown sugar
100g. (4 oz.) butter
essence of lemon

Let the sugar melt in a saucepan over a low flame.

Beat the butter to a cream. Stir it into the liquid sugar and boil until a little of this mixture hardens when dropped into cold water.

Add some essence of lemon. Beat the mixture with a fork for a few minutes.

Pour on to a buttered tray, and when it is cool enough mark into squares. These will snap off when cold.

Tablet

This is another of the most practical of the traditional sweets to make at home. Coated with chocolate it would make an interesting petit four substitute. The best flavourings for this purpose would be a 15ml. spoon (tablespoon) of whisky liqueur or the juice and grated rind of an orange.

900g. (2lbs.) granulated sugar
450ml. (scant pint) thin cream or milk.

Bring the milk and sugar gradually to the boil in an enamelled saucepan, stirring constantly. Let it boil for a few minutes.

When it turns a soft putty-like consistency on being dropped into cold water (about 245°F, 118°C), remove from the heat and add the flavouring.

Put the pan in a basin of cold water and stir the mixture with a spoon, scraping it from the sides as it solidifies. Keep stirring until it is quite grainy, then pour it on to a buttered slab.

When it is firm enough, divide into portions with a knife, and when it is cold and set break these apart and wrap in greaseproof paper.

Chocolate Truffles with Whisky

Chocolate is hardly traditional, but fine quality chocolate for eating and cooking is now much easier to find in Scotland. It is essential to use fine malt whisky.

Boil the cream. Away from the heat, mix in half of the chocolate, chopped, and stir until smooth.

Add the whisky. Pour the mixture into a metal bowl and set it over iced water. Beat with a wooden spoon until it is thick and quite cool.

Pipe the mixture on to greaseproof paper in 2·5cm (1-inch) rounds. Chill until firm. Brush your hands with icing sugar and roll each round into a ball. Chill until firm.

Melt the remaining chocolate over a bain-marie, being careful not to overheat it. Put the cocoa in a tray in an even layer.

Dip each ball in the chocolate on the end of a fork. Immediately place it in the cocoa and sprinkle a little cocoa over it.

When the tray is almost full of truffles, shake it to ensure that they are evenly coated with cocoa.

When all of the truffles have been coated, chill them thoroughly on clean paper. They taste best when kept in a cool container for a week or two.

675g. (1¹/₂lb.) dark chocolate
300ml. (¹/₂ pint) double cream
175g. (6 oz.) cocoa
small glass whisky
icing sugar

8. Preserves-Keeping the Flavour

... after a dram of good wholesome Scots spirits, there is now the tea-kettle put to the fire, the tea-table and silver and china equipage brought in, and marmalade and cream. (1729)[1]

Perhaps it is the notorious 'sweet-tooth' of the Scots which has long made jams and preserves so popular, but certainly descriptions abound where such items grace the table. 'In the breakfast the Scots, whether of Lowlands or mountains, must be confessed to excel us. The tea and coffee are accompanied not only with butter, but with honey, conserves and marmalades,' wrote Dr Johnson.[2]

For centuries, conserves made from fruits were always 'jellies' rather than 'jams' – that is, they were made only from the juices of fruits and sugar. They were, on the whole, luxury items, although honey was a staple in the diet in many areas. Waverley, in Scott's novel, finds himself breakfasting in the sunlit mouth of a cave on 'a morning repast of milk, eggs, barley bread, fresh butter and honeycomb . . .'[3] From the eighteenth century on, orange marmalade featured in the diet on a regular basis, although the production of the conserve was known many years before that. And despite the many tales which link the origins of the name to a new dish cooked up for the young Mary Queen of Scots during an illness ('pour Marie ma malade'), there is hard evidence to show that the word is in fact much older.

The word is derived from the Latin *melimelum* and the Greek *melimelon*, meaning 'sweet apple' via the Portuguese *marmelada* (quince). The original quince preserve would have been made with honey or wine, while the word 'marmalade' in the English language could be applied to a conserve made with almost any kind of fruit – marmalade of cherries, marmalade of apricots and so on. 'Jam' began to come into use from the Arabic *jamad* or preserved fruit in the middle of

the eighteenth century, and from that time the word marmalade was applied to jams made with citrus fruits.

Jams were made all over Britain in the eighteenth century, but only on a domestic basis. Many grocers did sell these home-made preserves, often with a label on the jar to show who had made it. One such tradesman was James Keiller of Dundee, who in 1797 bought in a bargain lot of Seville oranges off a ship which had arrived at Dundee harbour. Later realising that the oranges were too bitter to eat, his wife Janet set about turning the fruit into marmalade. It proved so popular that she continued making the conserve on an ever-increasing scale.

One of the problems of orange marmalade production was its seasonality. No preservatives then being available, production was restricted to December and January, and to utilise their marmalade-making equipment, the Keillers started as a side-line to produce 'butter scotch', a tablet made with butter and sugar. The tablet was spread onto a marble slab, then cut by a large metal frame into the distinctive shape it still has today.

Keiller's jam factory thrived, and at its peak employed over 3000 people, making not just jams and marmalades but baked goods, too, pies, shortbread and Dundee Cakes. Recently the marmalade and jam side of the business was sold by the Barker and Dobson confectionery group to Rank Hovis MacDougall, moving the marmalade operation from its old Scottish home to a base in Manchester where the group already produces Robertsons preserves.

The big name in Scottish preserves these days is Baxters of Speyside, a firm founded in 1868 and still fiercely a family firm despite repeated attempts at take overs. The firm started as a grocery shop, but began to expand when the present Chairman's grandmother, Margaret, began to make jams in her own kitchen to sell in the shop. 'My mother was a slave to work who worked up to eighteen hours a

Opposite: Making jam is a major operation at Baxter's Fochabers factory.

(British Gas Scotland)

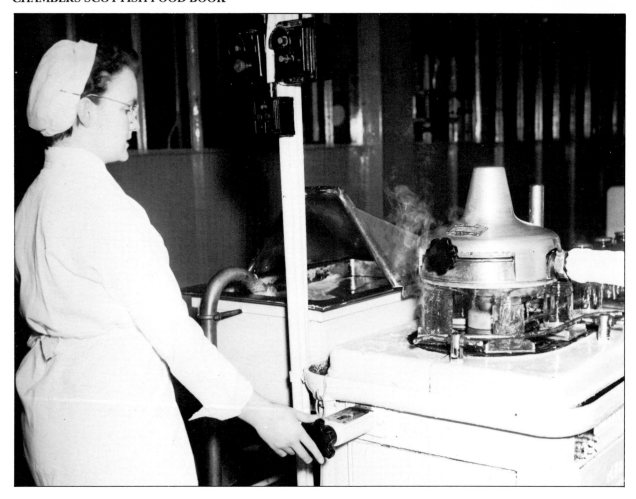

Above and opposite: Keiller's marmalade has enjoyed a considerable reputation, but the jam-making side of the business has now been moved to England.

(Keiller's)

day – she made three tons (3·048 tonnes) of blackcurrant jam two days before I was born,' says Gordon Baxter, who has been Chairman of the company since 1947.

The little store at Fochabers has grown considerably in the last hundred years, and now more than 150 000 people visit the factory premises every year. 'We are one of the very few producers who allow visitors,' says Gordon Baxter, 'and we are very proud of the fact that even our competitors come to see what we are doing.' The product range these days includes not just jams but the soups for which the company has become renowned (including the famous Royal Game Soup), cooking sauces and frozen seafood. Soups account for over half the business, while a bottled preserve, pickled beetroot, is a remarkably Scottish product, demand for which is only now beginning to creep south over the border.

Turn over is in excess of £40 million per annum, and the Baxters' jars and cans with their distinctive tartan design are enjoyed in more than 60 countries round the world. 'Our export trade is higher than in the rest of the industry,' says Gordon Baxter, 'and growing. But it still represents only twenty per cent of our business.'

The Baxter business is not by any means the biggest in the UK, but 'we are the best,' says Baxter. 'To stay that way we have to keep investing in the latest technology and skills.' Technology, however, would be nothing without quality food to work with. 'Our foods are the produce of the hills and glens,' says Baxter. 'Here at Fochabers we support a large infrastructure of food producers. Our salmon and game, our vegetables, and our raspberries and strawberries are all produced in Scotland, a high percentage locally.

'This country tends to an overproduction of jams and marmalades,' says Baxter, 'but the overproduction is at the cheap and cheerful end of the market – preserves made with imported fruit pulp. We aim for quality. We may not be big, but we are different and better.'

Arran Provisions, by contrast with Baxters, is a young company, and very much a growing one. Set up in 1981 by Ian Russell, their range of preserves is based on 'old family books on household management.'

The old recipes included many which Russell has re-popularised, such as their apple and thyme jelly, but the linchpin of Arran Provisions' success has been their special blends of mustard. 'Most of our supply of mustard seeds is grown on the island,' says Ian Russell, 'although if sales are exceptional we have to buy in from the East of Scotland. We are proud that our blends have been described as "the caviar of mustards". They are produced very differently from the classic French mustards, because in France they take out the essential oils for use in the perfume industry. On Arran we have a process whereby we bruise the seeds, retaining the essential oils. We then add certain spices and herbs, not through a cooking process, but a mixing process. Our mustards are not hot; we describe them as high usage mustards.'

Arran Provisions has grown rapidly from a small cottage industry using old-fashioned open-pan techniques to a thriving business in a smart new industrial unit. Much of their produce is exported to many corners of the globe, and they have been fortunate in that their mustards have appealed to the chilled food trade where it is incorporated into items such as mustard sauce for smoked mackerel.

Besides the giants of the jam industry such as Baxters of Speyside and Keiller's of Dundee, and old established names such as Scott's of Carluke (who now specialise in the presentation pack market), small companies like Arran Provisions have still managed to find a market. Another small company with a range of chutneys, mustards and marmalades is Galloway Lodge Preserves run by Norman Lennox. But Mr Lennox's main interest lies not in oranges or mustard seed, but in honey. Heather Hills Honey Farm north of Blairgowrie is the largest of six commercial bee farms in Scotland, and only twenty or so in the UK. (A beekeeper has fewer than 40 hives, a bee farmer 40 or more.) The farm buildings in fact house only the extraction and storage plants: the bees are kept near their food supply.

Heather Hills produces only set 'Blossom' and 'Heather' honey. 'Blossom honey is creamy, soft and white, and fairly sweet,' explains Norman Lennox. 'Heather honey is more tangy, although you can differentiate between the bell heather honey of July, which has a healthy taste, and the ling heather honey of August and September, which is tangy and has a distinct aroma.'

Once the overwintering period is over, the bees are moved to oilseed rape fields, where they remain until early June. Then they are moved to Blairgowrie's many raspberry fields to feed on the blossom. When they are moved from the berries to the heather, the final 'blossom' honey is removed from the hives. The bee farmer must constantly check the hives, to remove full 'supers' (the wooden frames containing the honeycombs) and to ensure that there is a queen bee – and only one – in the hive. 'The job is simple,' says Lennox. 'It is to keep as many bees as possible in the hive and to prevent them swarming. Careful track is kept of the age of the queen, by marking her with a small coloured blob of paint on her back. Commercially a queen has a useful life of no longer than three years. Worker bees live only four to five weeks during the height of the honey season, and to replace them a queen must lay up to two thousand eggs a day.'

The beekeeper's job is, in fact, far from simple, for in addition to the obvious occupational hazards, the bee farmer is at the mercy of the weather. The wet summer of 1985 was a disaster on a massive scale. 'We had 1780 hives at the beginning of the season, but only 250 at the end. The previous year we produced 47 tonnes (46·26 tons) of honey, but in '85 only 16 tonnes (15·75 tons). The problem was that because of the wet the queens stopped laying early, and in addition spring was late in 1986. The bees simply couldn't live long enough, so they just died.' Such a problem is not easily solved, as it is not possible to import bees because

Students travel from all parts of the world to learn about beekeeping.
(Heather Hills Honey Farm)

SECTIONS

OIL SEED RAPE HONEY

FOOD STORE

of problems with disease. New bees must therefore be bred, and though their number can theoretically be doubled every year, the breeding rate must be balanced against production levels, for divided hives produce less honey.

Extraction at Heather Hills is a mechanised affair, though timing is essential, especially with honey from oilseed rape which sets very quickly. 'An ideal comb is well sealed with beeswax to keep the honey inside fresh. The "capper" removes this wax film (the "cappings") and releases the honey. A centrifugal spinner takes the supers and slaps the honey against its wall as it spins, cleaning out the comb thoroughly and effectively. It is then passed via a filter into holding tanks, from where it is put into barrels and filtered once more, finally, into Heather Hills' distinctive beehive jar.'

Quality, says Lennox, relates to texture and taste. 'If the honey has not been properly extracted it will be grainy. It should be smooth and creamy. Heather honey tends to be granular, so it has to be blended with one part blossom honey to give it a creamier texture. If it lacks a distinctive aroma, you will know that too much other honey has gone into it.' The quality of Heather Hills' honey has certainly been praised in the past:

> When Strathardle bees make honey from raspberries it is of a markedly fine grain. The quality is then transferred, by some seeding process, in the comb to the heather honey . . . as a result Heather Hills Honey Farm honey is of an especially soft and delicate texture . . . all his honey is sold in the creamed state, and his honey is of a rare, soft, creamy texture, with the full flavour of heather nectar. I never tasted better.[4]

Honey is, it is claimed, one of the best and most natural of foods available. 'Honey is the most easily digested of all sugars, and bacteria cannot survive in honey, so there is no doubt that it is a wholesome food,' confirms Lennox. Certainly in these days of chemicals and additives, it is refreshing to know that there are still some foods which man does not think he can improve upon!

1. F. Marian McNeill, *The Scots Kitchen*, Blackie and Son, 1929 (1961 edition), London and Glasgow, p. 72.
2. *Ibid.*, p. 73.
3. Sir Walter Scott, *Waverley*.
4. Extract from an article in *The Scots Magazine*.

The Royal Highland Show is the highlight of the year for competitive honey makers. Bees prove a popular attraction.

(Carter Rae)

Seville Orange Marmalade

No Scottish cookery book would be complete without a recipe for marmalade. The same may be true of haggis and porridge, which symbolised our gift for thrift, but marmalade says more about us. It reminds us of our international spirit and of our flair and inventiveness. In culinary terms we had lost these qualities in the first half of this century. Now, happily, they are reappearing in a new generation of creative cooks. This is an adaptation of Meg Dods' recipe, as given by F. Marian McNeill, who wisely reminds us that marmalade is good with roast pork, duck and goose and with hot ham.

900g. (2lb.) Seville oranges
2 lemons
900g (2lbs.) sugar

Wipe the oranges and grate the peel lightly.

Cut the oranges in half then squeeze and sieve the juice.

Scrape the pulp from the inner skins and remove pips.

Boil the skins until tender. When cool, remove the white pulp from the skins. Cut the skins into narrow strips or chips.

Boil the chips, pulp and juice for ten minutes, add the juice of the lemons. Skim and boil for a further 20 minutes.

Pour into warm pots and cover when cold.

Rowan and Crab Apple Jelly with Thyme

The proportions of berries and apples are unimportant, and indeed the method is applicable to many fruits, for instance quince, which is equally savoury. These jellies are good with roast meats, apple and thyme making a particularly pleasing combination with pork.

Wash the fruit. Remove the stalks from the rowans, chop the apples roughly and put them together in a large pan. Cover with water and simmer until the fruit is tender.

Blanch the thyme in boiling water. Remove the stalks and chop the leaves.

Strain the juice into a jelly bag or muslin and allow juice to filter through. Be careful not to press on the fruit.

Measure the juice and return to the pan with the sugar. Stir over a low heat until the sugar is dissolved.

Boil until the jelly reaches setting point, stirring occasionally (test by allowing a little to cool on a saucer from time to time).

Add the thyme, pour into heated jars and cover.

900g. (2lbs.) rowans, picked just before they ripen fully
900g. (2lbs.) crab apples
large bunch of thyme
450g. (1lb.) sugar for each 600ml. (pint) of juice

Bramble Jelly

Bramble jelly is the most versatile and delicious of preserves. Perfect with Aberdeen butteries, pancakes and fresh bread, it is also the ideal sweetening ingredient for sauces to accompany game or pork. Its only rival is jelly made with damsons, those intense, black and sour little plums.

Wash the fruit and put them in a large pan with enough water almost to cover them. Boil until the fruit is well softened and the juice has a strong colour.

Strain the juice through a jelly bag or muslin, being careful not to press on the fruit.

Measure the juice. Add the sugar and stir over a low heat until the sugar has dissolved.

Boil until the jelly thickens visibly (about 30 minutes).

Pour into warm pots and cover immediately.

2·7kg. (6lbs.) brambles
450g. (1lb.) sugar for each pint of juice

121

Home Preserved Wild Mushrooms

The discovery that Scotland is rich in wild mushrooms is one of the most exciting things to have happened in the course of the culinary renaissance. In wet summers a glut of chanterelles is not uncommon, though a glut of cèpes is too much to hope for. A useful rule of thumb is to eat the best specimens, bottle the second best and dry everything else. Be *absolutely* sure of the identification of the mushrooms. Never experiment, not only because it is dangerous but also because only a few species are worth eating – cèpes, chanterelles, morilles, horn of plenty and oyster mushrooms are best, and all can be preserved.

To bottle mushrooms

Cèpes must be cut up to ensure they are free of maggots. Chanterelles never contain maggots. Wash and dry the mushrooms carefully. Fry them in good olive oil over a moderate heat, allowing them to expel most of their moisture, but being careful not to continue too long or they will toughen (about 5 minutes is usually right). No seasoning or other flavouring is necessary.

Sterilise Kilner jars and fill each at least half full. Follow the instructions for the use of the type of jar you have available. Boil the jars in water coming half way up their sides for 1½ hours. Allow to cool, then tighten the lids. Preserved in this way, mushrooms will keep for years.

To use them, first fry them briskly in a frying pan then season and employ them as you would fresh mushrooms (this frying is very important, to rid the mushrooms of any sliminess of texture).

To dry wild mushrooms

This is only really worthwhile for cèpes and morilles. Cut the mushrooms into thin strips, removing any spoiled areas.

Set them to dry on a rack placed over a central heating boiler or radiator, or in a very low oven with the door ajar. The former method is best, as the mushrooms can be left for a day or two in order to ensure that they are totally dry. They will keep almost indefinitely.

To use, soak the mushrooms in water for 30 minutes or until they are tender. Squeeze them dry, fry in oil or butter and add to sauces or soups. The flavour is very intense. Dried cèpes transform potato and beef dishes, morilles are wonderful with veal or chicken.

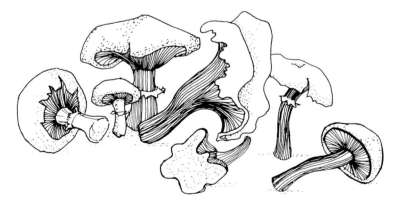

Honey Cakes

Honey was less used in the cookery of the past than one might expect. Cranachan (p. 76) is a notable exception. So are these little biscuits.

Melt the sugar with the honey in a saucepan and add the other ingredients. Mix well.

Roll out the paste about 1·5cm (½ inch) thick. Bake in a moderate oven (Gas 2, 300°F, 150°C) for 15 minutes.

When cool, cut into individual triangles or rectangles.

675g. (1½lb.) flour
325g. (¾lb.) honey
225g. (½lb.) caster sugar
100g. (¼lb.) mixed lemon and orange peel, cut in small dice
12g. (½ oz.) powdered ginger and cinnamon

Raspberry Syrup

Here is a recipe that is simplicity itself, but which can be adapted for all sorts of different uses. The most obvious, perhaps, is to use it as a concentrated fruit juice, to be served diluted with water (try a sparkling mineral water), and a sprig of mint. It can be served as a sauce for many desserts – as a striking contrast to a chocolate *marquise*, for example – or as a base for all manner of delicious fruit puddings. Note the similarity to the recipe for autumn fruits in claret (p. 77). Other fruits can be stewed briefly in the wine and sugar mixture, minus the raspberry juice, to great effect – plums would be my own favourite.

Marinate the raspberries in the wine for 2–3 days.

Sieve the liquid into a saucepan. Add the sugar, and bring to the boil, stirring constantly. Simmer for about 5 minutes.

When the syrup is cool, decant or filter into clean bottles and seal tightly. It will keep almost indefinitely in the refrigerator.

To make about 2 pints:

450g. (1lb.) raspberries
1 bottle red wine (preferably Bordeaux)
900g. (2lb.) sugar

123

Select Bibliography

Catherine Brown, *Scottish Regional Recipes*, Glasgow 1981.

E. H. M. Cox, *A History of Gardening in Scotland*, London 1935.

Catherine Lucy Czerkawska, *The Fisherfolk of Carrick*, Glasgow 1975.

A. Fenton, *Traditional Elements in the Diet of the Northern Isles of Scotland*, Lerwick 1976.

Theodora Fitzgibbon, *A Taste of Scotland*, London 1970.

T. Redford Franklin, *A History of Scottish Farming*, Edinburgh 1952.

William Gibson, *The Herring Fishing – Stronsay*, vol. 1. BPP 1984.

Lord Home, *Border Reflections*, London

Annette Hope, *A Caledonian Feast*, Edinburgh, 1987.

F. Marian McNeill, *The Book of Breakfasts*, Edinburgh 1975.

F. Marian McNeill, *The Scots Kitchen*, London and Glasgow 1929.

Patrick Rance, *The Great British Cheese Book*, London 1982.

David Stephen, *Highland Animals*, Inverness 1974.

Pat Thomson, *Take one Glen – recipes from glen kitchens*, Montrose 1973.

G. Kenneth Whitehead, *Deer Stalking in Scotland*, London 1964.

Index